JADED

Jaded

HOPE FOR BELIEVERS WHO HAVE GIVEN UP ON CHURCH BUT NOT ON GOD

A. J. Kiesling

Baker Books

A Division of Baker Book House Co
Grand Rapids, Michigan 49516

© 2004 by A. J. Kiesling

Published by Baker Books
a division of Baker Book House Company
P.O. Box 6287, Grand Rapids, MI 49516-6287
www.bakerbooks.com

Printed in the United States of America

Library of Congress Cataloging-in-Publication Data
Kiesling, Angela.
    Jaded : hope for believers who have given up on church but not on God / A. J. Kiesling.
        p.   cm.
    Includes bibliographical references.
    ISBN 0-8010-6467-8 (pbk.)
    1. Ex-church members. 2. Spirituality. I. Title.
BV820.K54 2004
253—dc22   2003026160

To my mother, who first taught me
what it means to believe

Contents

Acknowledgments

No book springs out of a vacuum. Like any endeavor worth undertaking, the shaping of words and thought into a book involves many, and here are the people I most want to thank for their involvement with *Jaded:*

Brian Peterson, for hearing the heart-cry behind my proposal and having the courage to present it before the Baker acquisitions committee.

My beloved editors' group of faithful friends and fellow wordsmiths: Marcia Ford, Debbie Cole, Melissa Bogdany, and Rhonda Sholar. You bring clarity, purpose, and sanity to this solitary path of writing I've chosen.

Kristin Kornoelje and the Baker editing team for your sharp eyes and insightful input; Karen Campbell and her marketing cohorts, along with Shanon Underwood and Paige Harvey, for expressing enthusiasm over a project that will undoubtedly prove to be controversial; Don Stephenson for capturing the vision of *Jaded* with such passion and zeal; and Dwight Baker, for taking a chance on an unknown author.

Kate and Emily Kiesling, for being the best gift in the world to me; my sister, Janet Angelo, for your encouragement; and my mother, Faye Ruth, for leading a life of never-waning faith and being my biggest fan.

Ken Davis, James Barron, and the other people who contributed stories to the pages of this text. Without you, the collective story of *Jaded* would not be told, but because of you many other "jaded believers" may find their way to a new understanding of God's grace.

Introduction

Divine Discontent

My first hint that this story needed telling arrived quietly, like an unexpected piece of mail, on a Sunday morning in 2000. It was the second week in a row I had opened the Yellow Pages to find a new church. *Where do I begin,* I wondered, as I scanned the names of hundreds of churches. When I narrowed that day's search to a small church in my community, I thought, *Well, Lord, who knows? Maybe this will be the one.* But two hours later, as I slipped out the sanctuary doors and made like a missile for my car, I mentally ticked off my twelfth church try. And then it happened. Tears, as unwanted as this frustrating quest I was on, coursed down my cheeks. Tears! Despite my disappointment with churches—ranging from heavy-handed pastors to a weariness with programs—I had a strong faith. God knew I wasn't going anywhere and, fortunately, I knew, neither was he. So why the tears?

A phone call to a friend later that week dropped the first piece of the puzzle into place. When I told her about my experience, she not only could relate but said the same thing had happened to her. Over the ensuing months, through other conversations, e-mail communications, and casual encounters with people I knew and didn't know, a common refrain began to emerge. Many, many people were sick and tired of church. Some were downright weary of it. But here was the catch: These were not "backsliders," people who had let faith take a backseat in their lives. These were men and women with a vibrant faith—God-seekers all, but souls with a deep thirst for more than the institutional church was offering. The yearning ran deep, like veins of gold in a mine that reach downward into some unknown core. Some of those believers, like me, still slogged away every Sunday morning, trying to find a place where they fit. Others left congregations in a storm of discontent. Still others stepped quietly through the back door and never came back. Most of them eventually found spiritual food and fellowship else-where. That "elsewhere"—both the where and why of it—is the subject of this book.

During my research I stumbled onto a phrase that captures the heartbeat of this message: *divine discontent.* Revolutions, whether social or spiritual, are always preceded by a collective restlessness, a heart-cry for something more. Could it be that God is stirring a divine discontent within the heart of his people, preparing them for much more than the staid, program-centered state of Western Christianity? That question begs a disclaimer. Certainly many believers, some of whom I know personally, still experience a freshness in their congregations and wouldn't dream of leaving the institutional church. Like-wise, many churches have found a way to be relevant to the changing culture—and especially to the emerging generation of young believers who demand authenticity above all else. My theme centers on those who find themselves riding the coat-tails of mainstream Christianity after years of participation. Black sheep in the fold.

Once I realized a powerful groundswell of jaded believers stirred the landscape, the untold story behind that spiritual surge kept me up at nights. It stole into my daytime thoughts as I worked on other writing projects. Suddenly, everywhere I went I bumped into similar stories. I went online and visited sites such as Beliefnet.com, where I discovered even more stories of a common thread. Surprisingly, an undercurrent of excitement fed this groundswell. Though church burnout was usually the catalyst, people's individual stories resonated with themes of grace, realism, and a spiritual vitality they had never known before. Weren't those three things hallmarks of classic Christianity? Did they not strike a chord deep within and hint at the abundant life Jesus talked about? If God was up to something, it was something wonderful indeed.

There's nothing new about the call for change within the church. That subject has been treated by scores of writers much more qualified than I. My intent is not to offer a scholarly treatise on church-weary believers but to do what my background as a journalist allows me to do best—tell their stories. Journeys of any kind are fraught with uncertainty and implicit excitement; spiritual journeys are no different. When the wayfarer returns, others always want to know: What was it like? Whom did you meet along the way? Was the terrain difficult? And, perhaps, most of all: *Was it worth the trip?* In a very real sense, our spiritual journeys won't be completed in this earthly life, so we can't "return" in the manner of one who embarks on a physical journey. But we can tell others about our experiences along the way. Word-of-mouth communication is more potent than any scholarly report or compiled data—and much more convincing. When Jesus healed a blind man on the Sabbath, the Pharisees accused Jesus of being a sinner. The blind man's response is unforgettable: "I know nothing about that one way or the other. But I know one thing for sure: I was blind . . . I now see" (John 9:25 MESSAGE).

The testimony of someone who has crossed over from spiritual burnout to a vibrant awareness of *who he or she is in Christ*—what the apostle Paul called "the simplicity that is

13

in Christ" (see 2 Cor. 11:3)—is no less miraculous. *What is their secret?* we wonder. *How did they break out of the wilderness zone?* And often, beneath the questions, lies a whispered prayer: *God, let that happen to me too!*

Homeward Bound

It's been said you have to leave home to find it. Over the past several years I've wondered: *Does the same hold true for God?* Like so many others who cut their baby teeth on Christianity, for me the path to "finding God" was signposted like a suburban freeway. Go to church, memorize Bible verses, pray and confess my sins daily, respond to at least one altar call—and never forget that God was watching my every move. I thought if I did all those things, I was guaranteed a spot in heaven. My reward here on earth would be the joy that comes from living what Jesus called the "abundant life."

The only problem with this formula for abundant living is that it doesn't work. Sooner or later you may find that out. Sometimes it's the church-mill that wears you down. Or perhaps a personal crisis leads to spiritual lethargy. You still believe in God; you go through all the right motions; you might even look convincing. But all the while you're dying a slow death on the inside, shouting a wordless cry to God: "Why isn't this Christianity thing working?"

Believers who are tired of "12 steps to spiritual growth" are faced with a puzzling question. They believe the words of Jesus and know they hold life-changing power. But how do those words "work" after the wear and tear of *everydayness* has dulled the glow of belief, after "churchianity" has replaced true Christianity, after spiritual idealism has turned into been-there cynicism?

In his book *Your God Is Too Safe* (Multnomah, 2001), author Mark Buchanan uses the phrase "chronic spiritual fatigue" to describe this malaise. When I first read his words,

I thought, *He's talking about me.* I find I'm not alone. Everywhere I turn I run into fellow believers so jaded on institutional church life they rarely bother to darken the doors of those hallowed spaces anymore. Or they begin a search for a place that fits—a place that offers more than just programs. A place that encourages those deep, sometimes dark, questions that accompany any meaningful spiritual quest. A place that won't cast believers aside when they encounter their own dark night of the soul. For some, that place may be a house church, a Bible study, a coffeehouse meeting, or something as simple as breakfast with another believer once a week.

Spiritual fatigue wears many different faces, and we may find ourselves in this slough of the soul as a result of a number of catalysts:

- a world-weariness that replaces the first spark of belief over time
- scars inflicted by fellow believers or pastors
- a life crisis that casts God in a bad light
- the existence of pain and suffering in a supposedly God-ordered world
- a growing awareness that what's preached from the pulpit doesn't always work in reality
- a despair that we'll never break out of churchianity into abundant life

At the same time, I've discovered something wonderful. Once God marks you as his own, he doesn't let go lightly. You can walk away from church, but you can't walk away from *him* so easily. If it were left to us, we'd have given up the struggle a long time ago. It's too hard, we sigh. And just when we think he'll finally leave us alone—let us quietly dissolve into our gray existence—he shakes things up again. Or frustrates our carefully wrought plans. Or speaks to us through the most unlikely characters.

15

That's what happened to me. In the midst of my own wilderness experience, God spoke to me through a paper sheep.

One afternoon, while facing a brutal deadline at my job, I realized I was about to crack. I shut the door to my office and "took five." After collecting myself, I made the short trip down the hall to the break room. Finding it populated with cheerful coworkers, I ducked into the bathroom for sanctuary instead. (I wonder how many people pray from bathroom stalls?)

After a few minutes I went back to my office and saw a new pile of folders on my desk. Folders that weren't there when I left. *Another stack of pages to be proofed,* I thought wearily. I started to dump them on top of the stack already growing on my desk, but something stopped me. On the top folder, penned on a white sticky note shaped like a sheep, was my first name. The production manager happened to have a packet of sticky notes shaped like sheep and had jotted my name on one to indicate which stack belonged to me. But in doing so she became the unwitting messenger of a mini-miracle.

It's funny how little things can catch you by surprise. God has been called the Hound of Heaven because of his endless, loving pursuit of us. Now that Hound was jerking my chain—gently. A bit of Scripture memorized in childhood Sunday school seeped into my tired brain: "I am the good shepherd; I know my sheep and my sheep know me" (John 10:14 NIV).

Later that evening, I opened my Bible and turned to the familiar chapter. The words leaped off the page: "I give them eternal life, and they shall never perish; *no one can snatch them out of my hand*" (John 10:28 NIV, emphasis mine). After that, I posted a cutout picture of a sheep on the bulletin board next to my computer; I make it a point to look at that sheep several times a day. It's there to remind me of how God sees me.

As sheep are wont to do, I had wandered from his side in the past few years, hopped over the fence, and free-ranged into unknown territory. Now he had come looking for me, and I was caught in that strange grip between wanting to run toward, and at the same time away, from him. If this parable were merely about enduring stress at work, it would have ended there. But the parable ran along much deeper lines, and I knew it instinctively—the way you always know when God is busy writing new text on the pages of your life. He wasn't finished with my story yet. He's not finished with yours either.

Jesus told stories; they made his teachings relevant and caused people to respond to him. Deep down we all love stories—especially good ones. Why else do we feed our dollars to the movie industry like quarters in a parking meter? Stories are the essence of the human experience. Stories are about *us*. Jesus did something else that caused people to respond to him. He met them on their own turf. He didn't expect prostitutes to dress like altar guild ladies before he'd talk to them. He didn't reproach partyers for swilling strong wine and telling crude jokes. He offered them a different life and left the choice up to them. When he spoke, his words transcended earthly authority, compelling the listeners to *do something* with what they'd heard.

In keeping with the pattern Jesus used, this book is told through stories—stories of real-life "sheep" who are tired of barnyard Christianity and yearn to break out and run behind the Shepherd on the high hills. Sheep who, for one reason or another, find themselves outside the institutional fold. In the following pages, you'll meet ordinary people who have embarked on extraordinary journeys beyond spiritual burnout to renewed spiritual vitality. Some are just discovering that place of rest. Some made the transition years ago and now point the way for others. My prayer is that, through their stories, you might see yourself and "meet" the Savior all over again. Only he can lead his travel-weary flock to green pastures, the secret place of *rest* that seems so maddeningly elusive to our formulaic way of thinking.

Although this book trains a spotlight on the house-church movement and other forms the postmodern church is taking, God is never one to be boxed in. He may not choose to transform the Western church through these means at all. Instead, he might see fit to revitalize the institutional church—with all its orthodox trappings intact—or, better yet, morph it into something we could not have foreseen.

Ultimately, *Jaded* is a chronicle of those whose path to God has taken not the highway but the byway—the roundabout route. The good news is that even the byway is bordered by grace.

1

ROCK-BOTTOM BELIEVERS

New Year's Eve 1988 was the night everything clicked for Wayne. As he held the small paper candleholder—issued to each of the faithful attending the church's Watch Night service—his mind wandered. The pastor's voice droned from the platform, creating a hazy backdrop for Wayne's thoughts. Minutes passed. Outside, someone leaned on a car horn and yelled out a party whoop to celebrate the turning of a new year. Jolted by the sudden noise, Wayne realized too late he had jiggled the candleholder, and a drop of hot wax spilled onto his hand.

A silent prayer took shape before the wax could harden: "Lord, why can't I be out there having fun? Does Christianity have to be boring?"

God's unconventional response surprised and delighted him. Wayne sensed the Lord inviting him to go outside and celebrate the New Year with him. That answer triggered an awakening in Wayne's spirit, which had dulled over the years of trying to live for God and be a "good Christian." The affirmation that God *simply wanted to be with him* seemed revolutionary.

As he drove home from the service, Wayne replayed images from the Gospel account of Jesus' first miracle. The Son of God had been at a wedding—a festive celebration with dancing and drinking—when the Father issued a quiet "Now!" that unleashed the divine spark into the world of men. That one act—turning water into wine—would resonate throughout the rest of time, marking Jesus as divinity in the midst of our humdrum existence. Yet he chose a party, of all places, to announce his divinity. Was there any significance to that?

If you ask Wayne today, he will assert unabashedly that there is. But, far from turning him into a freewheeling reveler, that spiritual awakening transformed him from a burned-out, jaded believer on the brink of suicide into a man whose faith lights up a room. Those who know Wayne know him as a person of laughter—and those who don't know him are not in his presence long before they hear the reason for his joy. But there's one key difference in the way he shares his faith today. Rather than Bible-thumping and emphasizing the need for repentance, he tells people about the amazing love of God and how it changed his life.

It's contagious and very effective. "I want to infiltrate churches with the good news I now know and infect them with a grace virus," Wayne says. Those raised in the church know the term "good news" to mean simply the gospel. Of course it's good news, we say defensively. Yet often people we meet experience it to be otherwise—largely because of the hypocritical, legalistic conduit it is sometimes delivered through. In his book *Soul Survivor: How My Faith Survived the Church,* Philip Yancey includes a riveting quote from one of Walker Percy's characters in *The Second Coming.* The character speaks for perhaps much of the Western world—and even a few church-weary saints: "I am surrounded by Christians. They are generally speaking a pleasant and agreeable lot, not noticeably different from other people. . . . I cannot be sure they don't have the truth. But if they have the truth, why is it the case that they are repellent precisely to the degree that they embrace and advertise the truth? . . . A mystery: If the good news is true, why is not one pleased to hear it?"

Yancey restates that last question and then adds: "Bible college professors insisted, 'We live not under law but under grace,' and for the life of me I could not tell much difference between the two states. Ever since, I have been on a quest to unearth the good news, to scour the original words of the gospel and discover what the Bible must mean by using words like *love, grace,* and *compassion* to describe God's own character. I sensed truth in those words, truth that must be sought with diligence and skill, like the fresco masterpieces that lie beneath layers of plaster and paint in ancient chapels."[1]

The good news—the gospel of grace—is indeed catching. As we talked over coffee at a bookstore café, Wayne couldn't keep his voice to a low pitch. His decibels increased with the momentum of his story, but the results were worth it. When he got up to leave, a young man sitting directly behind him jumped to his feet and stuck out his hand. "I couldn't help but overhear your story," he said, eyes shining. "I can relate to everything you talked about."

The young man said he yearned for a faith experience that matched the revolutionary, even mystical, union with God he had read about in the New Testament. Why couldn't he find that in churches? he wanted to know. Why had the very word *Christian* become a turnoff to so many?

Like most transitions, Wayne's spiritual burnout didn't happen overnight. Rather, it resembled the "frog in boiling water" phenomenon of change so gradual it was hard to detect until the damage was done. Things had started out so differently. In the early days of his faith-walk, Wayne never dreamed he'd one day nearly turn his back on God.

"When I first became a believer it was incredible," he recalls. "All my life I'd been to church, but suddenly there

21

was no more striving for God because he was right there. I was on a honeymoon with the Holy Spirit."

Growing up in a mainline denominational church, Wayne heard about grace, but the church also emphasized the need to measure up and "get right" with God. Wayne did his best to "get right with God" whenever he erred, but of course his best wasn't good enough.

"All these teachings mixed together in my head and started to make me weary, because the sin issue was never over with," he says. "I was taught that you had to perfect yourself in the flesh to be acceptable to God, even though we said we believed in grace. I'd had a glimpse of real grace when I was a teenager, but once I was inside the institution [church], everything was like '10 ways to be a Christian,' '25 ways to pray better,' what music to listen to, what music not to listen to. After a while I thought, *What's up with this?* I got to the point where I was closing out the world so much I was losing my mind."

After fourteen years inside what he calls "churchianity prison," Wayne reached a turning point. He had hit rock bottom. "I finally just said, 'Forget God.' If he's still counting my sins against me, I don't need him. People were constantly telling me I needed to get right. What is getting right? How do you know when you're finally right? All those years I never drank or smoked or went to bars. I thought my righteousness was first-class, but I was miserable."

Welcome to the Wilderness

Wilderness—it's a word that conjures up images of reality TV programs about rugged men and women surviving with nothing but their wits to guide them. For some it brings to mind biblical nomads, their headdresses flapping as they lean into the wind to follow God's cloud. But find yourself in a wilderness drift of the soul, and the picture changes dramatically. Suddenly the canvas is painted in dark hues. You discover the ground under your feet rocky, the way hard-going, and God silent. Yes, God—that once benevolent deity who called you to him—now seems to have disappeared.

As the 1990s gave way to the new millennium, the topic of spirituality heated up on all fronts. Sales of religion titles soared, prompting secular publishers who once scoffed at spirituality to sample a piece of the marketing pie. With the world careening toward the unknown, God drew ink from major newspapers and magazines, stirred conversation at coffee bars and college think tanks, and beckoned to us from highway billboards and the Internet. Suddenly God was in. People no longer looked at you funny if you mentioned his name in casual conversation. And the admission that you actually prayed about something was almost avant-garde.

Yes, the century of evangelicalism ended on a high note, and the new millennium promised to maintain that momentum. But while new churches sprouted like dandelions across North America—and spirituality-based websites dotted the digital landscape—a quiet change was taking place within the Christian infrastructure: Lifelong churchgoers bid farewell to the institutional church and found God through house churches, conversations at coffeehouses, monastic retreat centers, and even labyrinthine prayer walks.

None of this happened overnight. But by anybody's standard, the last third of the twentieth century witnessed enough changes to give church historians writer's cramp. Cradle mainstream churchgoers traded in their staid services for the charismatic renewal, leaving their home denominations in droves. The rise of "televangelism" ushered in the era of glam-gospel, replete with big-haired celebrity preachers and prosperity teaching (remember the "Me" generation?). After years of emotional/spiritual highs, many believers jaded on "charismania" chucked their too-lively congregations for traditional forms of Christian worship. Some flocked to new "liturgy lite" churches that combined traditional worship and symbolism with contemporary music and other cultural trappings. Others embraced Orthodox liturgies or headed for remote monasteries to experience the "cloister walk." Messianic Jewish fellowships cropped up, attracting Jews and Gentiles alike to their first-century-type church gatherings. And some former Protestants shocked their brethren by becoming Catholics.

Ironically, at the same time, the word *Christian* itself had become a loaded term. It's so tainted with images of TV money changers and Bible-thumpers that a whole generation of young Jesus-followers now avoids it like the plague. Books aimed at the Christian youth market often don't use the word *Christian*—even in sentences that refer to reading "Christian classics." Now those books are called spiritual classics or religion classics. Anything but Christian.

"That word turns them off," one editor said. "They hear the word *Christian* and immediately shut down." Paradoxically, those same young readers are excited about God and boldly identify themselves with Jesus. An earlier, best-selling book published by the company that editor works for provided hard evidence—in the form of bookstore sales—that these same readers are hungry to learn more about God. They just don't want it wrapped in Christian clothing.

It's safe to say that all this spiritual activity beams a spotlight on the deepest cry of every human heart—the longing for God, or the longing to fill that God-shaped vacuum of the soul Blaise Pascal wrote about. And when we don't find the source that can fulfill that longing, we invariably go looking.

The steps that follow a believer's honeymoon phase with God often lead straight into the wilderness. By definition a wilderness is a dry, bleak place—the kind of place you don't head into by choice. But it's also true that the wilderness is a proving ground. Having entered this barren place, you eventually emerge changed. Sometimes changed to the core.

In his novel *The Visitation,* author Frank Peretti tells of a burned-out pastor's first glimmering recollection of when things began to go wrong:

> By the time I reached my front door I felt nineteen again. Not young, just burdened with an old sorrow, a deep loneliness, a familiar despair.
>
> Certain smells, like the odor of your grade school or even the scent of an old girlfriend, remain in your memory forever. An old song can bring back the feelings you had when you first fell in love. You may think you don't remember how the back door of your childhood home sounded when it swung shut, but if you could hear it again, you would know the sound.
>
> As I sat on the couch and picked up my banjo, I knew this feeling. I knew when and where I'd felt it before. I was nineteen at the time, sitting alone on the bed in my room in Seattle. I still remembered the "new house" smell of that room, the texture of the Sears bedspread, the feel and color of the blue-green carpet on the floor, the exact position of my Glen Campbell poster on the wall. I had a banjo in my hands then too—a brown, fifty-dollar Harmony with a plastic resonator, and I could have been playing the same song I was playing now. . . .
>
> It was a pivotal moment, I suppose, frozen in memory like a historic photo from the *LIFE* magazine archives, a passage out of childhood and a painful end to illusions. I'd been in love, but lost the girl; I'd been a prophet of God, but proven wrong; I'd prayed for the sick, but they didn't get well; God had called me to a faraway city, but hadn't met me there; my friends and I were going to change the world for God, but they had all scattered after graduation. I had been a young man of such hope and faith, but now my hope and faith were gone, slowly suffocated by disappointment and disillusionment. . . .
>
> Jesus seemed far away, and strangely enough, I was content to leave him there. I didn't want to talk to him; I feared and distrusted anything he might say to me.

25

I was saved, sanctified, born-again, and Spirit-filled, but Jesus and I were strangers.[2]

Later in the book, Peretti paints an allegorical picture of the wilderness phase of spirituality. Through the mind of his protagonist, he likens this troubling bend in the road to leaving your childhood home. Mom and Dad stand on the porch watching as you walk down to the front gate, turn to look back, and wave before passing through to the world beyond. You know you can never return. You've stepped outside the boundaries of that place forever. You may long to return to the place of innocence, but you can't. You've changed, and you can't erase the new version of *you* that's come into being.

The good news, however, is that when you've hit rock bottom, the only way to go is up.

2

CALL ME ISHMAEL

If the spiritual stories of our lives could all be read in a book, we'd probably smile to see how similar the themes run. The backdrops would differ, as would major events and characters. But in each story I suspect we'd find one central theme: searching for God, searching for ourselves; finding God, finding ourselves; "losing" God, losing our way; and finally coming home again to the God who was there all along—but merely waiting for us to die to ourselves so we might fully grasp what the apostle Paul calls the "glorious riches of this mystery, which is Christ in [us]" (Col. 1:27 NIV).

But how does a person go about *dying* to self? For many of us, it's a nice Christian cliché. For others, it's found in the gritty art of self-determination: We claim to have "died" to self when we give up smoking or clench our jaw instead of verbally attacking someone. But in a sense, these are the easy sins to avoid. When the Holy Spirit sets up residence in our spirit and starts to "clean house," these obvious misdemeanors are the first to go. But then he puts the sickle to the weeds cropping up through the floorboards; he begins to pry up long-buried roots that threaten the foundation. Greed, pride, malice, lust, covetousness, deceit, a lying tongue behind smiling lips—these are the foul-smelling sins that fester down in the dank cellar. And they don't uproot easily.

Can believers "claim" their way to a clean spiritual slate? If we confess our sins often enough, will we somehow emerge squeaky-clean one day, relieved to see that all our efforts have finally paid off? Though few church leaders would admit it, contemporary Christian thought propagates this belief more often than not. We cloak it in biblical-sounding words, but the bottom line is the same error false religions commit: trying to earn our spiritual stripes by our own human efforts—even those rendered in the name of Jesus.

No wonder a tired flock of sheep has wandered back into the barnyard hungry, bleating, pathetic—yearning for one touch from the Great Shepherd.

So we rail against the heavens: Is this what we got saved for? Must there be this constant struggle? Is this all Jesus meant when he talked about the "abundant life"? If so, most of us could do without it. After all, our Western Christianity doesn't cost us very much these days—certainly not our lives, and often not even our pride. The answer lies metaphorically in something we shy away from: death.

A Swiss-born doctor named Elisabeth Kübler-Ross rocked the medical world in 1969 with her groundbreaking book *On Death and Dying*. Prior to its release, people "talked about death only in whispers and did their public grieving behind black veils," as one website rendered it. Their private grief was another matter—horribly real but not a subject open to discussion. Kübler-Ross rent the veil that separated private and public grief in her book. She made it okay to talk about death and dying and introduced what she called the Five Stages of Grief (or Dying) model. According to this model, dying people go through five distinct stages when they are told they have a terminal illness. The stages are denial, anger, bargaining, depression, and acceptance. Over time, psychologists and medical practitioners applied the grief model to other situations where someone suffers a loss or change in social identity.

As I compiled the stories for this book, it struck me that the grief model applies to the spiritual journey as well. We shouldn't be too surprised. Christ told us plainly we could expect "death" when we join ranks with him.

> I tell you the truth, unless a kernel of wheat falls to the ground and dies, it remains only a single seed. But if it dies, it produces many seeds. The man who loves his life will lose it, while the man who hates his life in this world will keep it for eternal life. Whoever serves me must follow me; and where I am, my servant also will be. My Father will honor the one who serves me.
>
> John 12:24–26 NIV

German clergyman and martyr Dietrich Bonhoeffer echoed this same thought when he said, "When Christ calls a man, he bids him 'come and die' "[1] Unlike Kübler-Ross's grief model, however, the fifth stage of spiritual "dying" is not intended to be a passive acceptance of a miserable condition. It is an awakening into a spiritual rest we've yearned for all the years of our faith-walk. While the wilderness is the place of spiritual death—and therefore, it could be argued, a viable part of the journey—the problem is that death doesn't sound like a pleasant proposition. We'd prefer to stay in our spiritual comfort zones, or at least prolong the inevitable dying for as long as we can. And by its very nature death is something that *happens* to you, not (excluding suicide) something you plan. Who among us would be brave enough to plunge willingly into the wilderness that marks our spiritual dying, the land of chronic spiritual fatigue?

God helps us—he gives us the push we need. It sounds cruel to our finite minds, but think of it this way. In his book *Making Sense Out of Suffering*, Peter Kreeft uses the analogy of a hunter who finds his dog caught in a bear trap in the woods. The hunter must push the injured paw a little farther in before releasing his animal from the jaws of death. Otherwise, he would tear the limb to shreds. In that painful moment when the dog teeters between trust in his master and fear of the unknown, anything could happen. But seconds later, as the master holds him in his arms and heads for home, the dog realizes he was safe all along.

For Wayne, the rock bottom of the wilderness phase occurred when he realized he couldn't muster the will to go to church one more time. "I remember coming to a point where I said, 'That's it.' I had just moved into an apartment with a friend named Jesse, who was also a believer. 'Jesse,' I said, 'don't talk to me about God. Don't ask me to go to church with you. I'm tired. I just want to be a roommate and nothing else.' I was sick of hurting God and told him to go ahead and throw me into hell. In fact, I fantasized about killing myself."

One night Wayne had a startling dream that he still remembers vividly. In the dream he was walking in a wheat field with another Christian. Suddenly, a breathtaking castle came out of the sky in the distance, and he watched as a line of people walked toward the castle door. As they stepped through the door, shining white robes fell on each one. Exhilarated, and wanting to reach the castle too, Wayne struggled to run ahead but couldn't. He woke up, his heart pounding in his chest. What had the strange dream meant?

When he fell back asleep, the same dream returned, only this time he was walking alone. He rushed toward the castle door, and as he stepped through the archway a shimmering white robe dropped on him—then he woke up.

"Over the next few weeks, the meaning of the dream became clear to me," Wayne says. "I believe the first time I tried to reach the castle, legalism or churchianity was walking with me. Only when I returned alone, in the simplicity of my faith in Christ, could I make it through."

Though he didn't know it then, Wayne was only a few days away from leaving the wilderness and entering a new phase of his spiritual journey—a place of unspeakable joy and rest. God had met him in the wilderness, and it was time to leave it behind. One week later he met a young lawyer from Louisiana who teaches, of all things, a gospel of grace. It was the heavenly drink Wayne had been thirsting for. (We'll return to Wayne's story in chapter 8.)

Belief, Interrupted

Doubts about God unfurl slowly, like the first leaves on a sapling planted too late in the spring. Though we expect salvation to usher us into a state of perfect belief and carefree existence, that is almost never the case. Even a cursory glance through the writings of great Christian thinkers underscores this disturbing truth.

Flannery O'Connor, a Southern writer known for dispensing truth in the form of shocking fictional stories and characters, wrote from a profound understanding of the mystery of faith. A devout Catholic, she returned to her family home in Georgia in 1951 when she discovered she had lupus. From that home she kept up a lively correspondence until her death in 1964. Her letter to one friend captures this sense of mystery behind the Scriptures:

> I think there is no suffering greater than what is caused by the doubts of those who want to believe. I know what torment this is, but I can only see it, in myself anyway, as the process by which faith is deepened. A faith that just accepts is a child's faith and all right for children, but eventually you have to grow [spiritually] as every other way, though some never do. . . .

31

My reading of the priest's article on hell was that hell is what God's love becomes to those who reject it. Now no one has to reject it. God made us to love Him. It takes two to love. It takes liberty. It takes the right to reject. If there were no hell, we would be like the animals. No hell, no dignity. And remember the mercy of God. It is easy to put this down as a formula and hard to believe it, but try believing the opposite, and you will find it too easy. Life has no meaning that way. . . .

Whatever you do anyway, remember that these things are mysteries and that if they were such that we could understand them, they wouldn't be worth understanding. A God you understood would be less than yourself.[2]

Bamboozled by a "Brother"

We may see "through a glass darkly" when it comes to God, as the apostle Paul said, but we expect to see our fellow believers through clear lenses in the here and now. Unfortunately, calamity often results when we do. For so many believers it is *other Christians* who prompt the nosedive into spiritual disillusionment—one of the triggers that lead many people to walk away from church. We joke about Christians being the only army that shoot their wounded, but the jest loses its humor when we find ourselves the brunt of it.

Joan's spiritual wilderness began on a fall day in a 7-Eleven parking lot. By all appearances, she was still on a honeymoon with God. The Jesus sticker plastered to her Corolla bumper boldly proclaimed her faith, and she attended church functions three times a week. Two years earlier she had abandoned the party lifestyle for Christianity. Never before had she felt such joy, peace, and contentment in life. Surrounded by other young believers whose faith seemed contagious, she was in love with Jesus. No longer was he just a name in the

Bible or a haloed baby in a plastic manger scene. Jesus was real. Christianity was real. Life was good.

A fender-bender at a 7-Eleven gas pump changed all that.

She honked, but it was too late. Joan watched helplessly as another car crunched the passenger door of her car. On her small salary, finances were already tight. Now she had a deductible to pay if she wanted to get the car door fixed.

"You should look for a body shop owned by a Christian," friends advised. "That way you can be sure of dealing with someone trustworthy." The father of a girl Joan taught in Sunday school owned a body shop and charged reasonable prices. He came recommended, so she booked an appointment and showed up on the scheduled day.

Located on the outskirts of town in an older, commercial district, the body shop was wedged between two dilapidated buildings that leaned lazily beneath cropped oak trees. A tall chain-link fence guarded the property. Joan steered the Corolla through the gate and parked beside a rumpled Chevy. A man with greasy hair came out from the shadows of the garage, a sliver of belly showing below his T-shirt.

"Can I help you?" he asked, wiping his hands on a rag.

"I'm looking for Mr. Wilcox," Joan said as she got out of the car. "I need my car door fixed."

"I'm Mr. Wilcox," the man said, his grin showing a gold tooth.

"You're Celeste's father?" As soon as the words were out she regretted them, her surprise sounding too obvious.

"That's right. She told me I could expect you," he said, his eyes traveling up and down Joan's body in one quick glance.

She showed him the damage to her car; he assured her he could fix the door without replacing the part and save some money in the process. "That way you can bless me at the same time," he said, taking a look at the total on the insurance check in her hand.

That last part confused Joan. Young and ignorant, she assumed his "blessing" would come in the form of business from a new customer. Three days later, when she went to pick up the car, Mr. Wilcox stood in the doorway to the garage's gloomy interior.

"Well, now. Look who it is," he said, his smile making her uneasy. He walked out to the lot, demonstrated how well the passenger door opened and closed on the repaired Corolla, then ambled back toward the office to settle the bill. Joan followed behind, mute.

"For a moment," she recalls, "I just stood there, waiting for him to present the paperwork."

"I have a word from the Lord for you," Mr. Wilcox said. "I'm a prophet of the Most High God. Give me your hand, and I'll tell you what the Lord is saying to you."

Joan had heard of prophets—not just the ones from the Bible but present-day men and women through whom God spoke today. Maybe Mr. Wilcox really did have a "word" for her. Friends at church had received personal words from God before. Now it must be her turn, she reasoned. Not wanting to appear rude, she let him grasp her hand.

From the distance of nearly twenty years, Joan says she doesn't remember the exact words he "prophesied" that day, but she does remember they were vague enough to apply to just about anyone. "When you're gullible and hungry to hear from God, it's easy to attach more meaning to words than is actually there," she says.

What she remembers most about the encounter is the creepy feeling the man gave her. As he ended his prophecy, he pulled on her hand, forcing her close to his chest for a "brotherly" hug. She pulled away, thanked him for the repair work, and left.

Only years later did she realize Mr. Wilcox not only invaded her personal space and planted a seed of suspicion within her about so-called men of God, he essentially stole

$350 from her—in the form of unused excess on an insurance check.

Two Ishmaels

For Joan, the incident with Mr. Wilcox passed, and she took it in stride. But even now, she says, it stands out in her memory as the first time she linked God with the unsavory character of his children. Without making a conscious decision to do so, she put up a filter in her soul to screen everything that went by the name of *Christian.*

"I would be ready, and much more watchful, the next time," she says. "Or so I thought. Over time, more serious incidents etched chinks in my spiritual armor. I never even realized when I passed from spiritual innocence to cynicism. Only hindsight, and the wisdom that comes from spiritual growth, allows you to separate God from the actions of those who claim to represent him. And only hard-won spiritual maturity brings us to a place where we begin to understand just how amazing grace is."

By the time she began to piece together a divine pattern to the events of her life, Joan realized how that autumn day at the body shop served as a jumping-off point for a downward spiral. The carefree days were over. Welcome to the wilderness.

"Like the biblical Ishmael, I had been born into a wonderful promise, only to find myself thrust into the desert and banished to a life of wandering. At least that's what I thought," she recalls. "Would God meet me in the wilderness as he had met Jesus, after testing the mettle of his spirit? Or would I be forced to face the darkness alone?"

God promises he will never give us more than we can bear, but there come times in every life when those words seem to be a mockery. Other troubling events awaited Joan as she took her first halting steps into the wilderness. Though she didn't know it then, she would also become a type of that other Ishmael—the *Pequod* deckhand of *Moby Dick* who survived a wreck at sea, paddled to shore in a coffin, and lived to tell the tale.

3

THE CHURCH'S BACK DOOR

As much as church leaders cringed to hear it, social scientists and religion researchers predicted the quiet exodus of believers from churches in the last decade of the twentieth century—and continuing into the twenty-first century. George Barna of the Barna Research Group has stated, "During the '90s, truly a period of contradictions and paradoxes, we saw a simultaneous increase in people's openness to religion and decrease of personal involvement in religious activities. Church attendance dropped to about 4 out of 10 adults attending on any given Sunday, and among church attendees, the norm went from three appearances per month down to two." Whereas in 1991, 49 percent of adults attended church services, that figure had dropped to 40 percent by 2000 and is expected to decrease to 35 percent by 2010.[1] Another sobering aspect of church attendance statistics is how little of so-called church growth is a result of new converts. Most churches that claim healthy growth are merely seeing new attendees come through the front door of their church after leaving the back door of another church—sometimes just down the street.

Bred into a world of consumerism, many Western believers have adopted the mind-set that churches exist to serve them, not the purposes of God. Or, as Barna puts it, "If it takes too long, requires too much effort, costs too much money, seems too complicated or causes too much discomfort, then the chances are good it won't make the day's agenda."[2] Indeed, a "utilitarian" attitude prevails in postmodern American culture, among both churched and nonchurched individuals, asserts Princeton University social sciences professor Robert Wuthnow. That utilitarianism is characterized predominantly by the question, What's in it for me? In an odd twist, Wuthnow states that many sermons and church publications blatantly express this idea—for example, in calling on people to serve others because it will make them feel good.[3]

Some have even likened our culture's obsession with consumer Christianity to the "McDonald's" mentality. Writing via a church website, United Methodist pastor Benjamin S. Sharpe asserts:

In our society McDonald's has become the epitome of the consumer experience. This successful fast-food chain has learned that to appeal to consumers one must offer many menu choices designed to please a variety of different tastes and appetites. The choices cannot cost too much. Also the restaurant realizes that it must not entangle the customer with any intimacy or relationships. So at McDonald's the customer does not have to form a relationship with a waiter or waitress—just step up to the counter, order, and walk away.

In western culture, the Church is becoming "McDonald-ized" in order to retain parishioners who are enslaved to consumerism. We try to offer what McDonald's does: We provide lots of menu choices designed to please the appetites and personal tastes of many different individuals.

We try to hold down the price of commitment in time and money. We remove the inconvenience of intimacy. This is why many people love the megachurch environment where they can be anonymous consumers. In such a setting one never has to get to know anyone else!

McChristianity. The Barna research group has revealed that the vast majority of Americans consider themselves to be Christians. Yet we are a nation of McChristians who expect the Church to pander to our appetites while requiring minimal commitment in return. Like the multitudes who turned away from Jesus when he presented himself as the living bread that came down from heaven, we do not have the appetite for radical intimacy with God (cf. John 6:53-66).[4]

Sharpe breaks it down even further, spelling out the red flags that betray our entrance into the ranks of consumer Christianity. Specifically, he states, we are Christian consumers when we:

- Want lots of choices from a menu of programs that appeal to our personal tastes and preferences.
- See ourselves as individuals who have no intimate relationship with others in the body of believers.
- Believe the reason for the church's existence is to meet our felt needs, providing a product or service.
- Leave when we don't feel like we are getting our money's worth or proper service.
- Create a personal motto of "Ask not what I can do for God, but what the church can do for me."
- Base our loyalty on whether our felt needs are met.[5]

Certainly this consumer mind-set accounts for a good portion of the church dropout rate, whether we like it or not. Jill, a successful writer and executive assistant, admits that being spoiled by the best of churches can make other churches appear glaringly lacking, especially when a person moves into a new area and struggles to find the right church "fit." That's what happened to Jill and her husband. When they moved to a large Southern city that offered hundreds of churches, she and Brian struggled to find a church. After visiting several, they finally found one that felt right, but a move across town—a distance of thirty-five miles—necessitated finding another church. They tried out a handful of area churches but never found anything that "clicked," as Jill puts it.

"In the past, we'd attended some churches that set the benchmark really high. For instance, we tried one small community church near us," she says. "It was the type of church where the minister will stand up front and shake your hand as you leave. What it lacked in depth and professionalism, it would make up for in friendliness and warmth, we reasoned. But hardly anybody came up to us and said boo. We had been spoiled to really deep teaching, awesome praise and worship, and a sense of community. We tried another church, but during a sermon the pastor talked about the church debt and how they'd have to make layoffs among the staff. That hit Brian and me the wrong way. The church was in a brand-new facility, located on prime real estate. They had spent tons of money on it, so my first question was, Did they simply not project right? Why were they suddenly announcing debt problems and asking people to give? We could have gone there anyway and asked questions later, but I was too tired. Too tired. In the end we came full circle back to the fellowship we loved across town. The downside is that we're not able to get involved with small groups because of traffic and the distance. We typically go once a week and benefit a lot from the teaching. I know we should be more service-oriented, but right now that's not possible."

Though Jill never became a church dropout, she can understand how believers get to that point. "When we first moved here, it was kind of a joke," she says. "We went to so many churches I feel like I could have started a church. Because there's so much effort in finding a church you feel comfortable in, I can see how people would finally just say, 'Forget this.'" She points to certain approaches that are instant turnoffs for many, such as pastors sitting onstage in big throne chairs or long announcements that eat up valuable teaching time. "These are really little things that sound silly, but it all boils down to style—what style you're comfortable with."

Jill believes theological differences, personality differences, worship preferences, and other criteria account for why one person might feel instantly at home in a church while another walks through the door and just as quietly walks out.

A person who appreciates intellectual teaching in church, Jill claims her longtime church home—the church that set the benchmark so high—did a great job of blending old and new. "Never in my life had I recited the Nicene Creed or the Apostles' Creed," she says. "Yet there were some very contemporary things going on at that church too. They might sing an old hymn of the faith and then a song by Steven Curtis Chapman."

Jill thinks that some believers may have to compromise in their search for a church that fits. "It really is a dilemma, because if you've been to a church that hits this benchmark and you move to a new community where nothing matches that benchmark, what do you do? If you drop out for an extended time, you have to be very disciplined and still be in fellowship."

When asked what she would do if faced with that dilemma, Jill says she'd look into starting a home group. Her job at a busy Christian television headquarters woke her up to the reality of how many people now look to the visual media—both television and the Internet—for their spiritual sustenance. "It's interesting how many people will write and say we're their spiritual food. Some are shut-ins, some are in prison, but some are just burnt out on church."

41

Backdoor Believers

Of the five generational groups in society—Seniors (1926 and before), Builders (1927–1945), Boomers (1946–1964), Busters (1965–1984), and Mosaics (1985–2004)—the older two groups are the more likely to cling to the traditional church. Raised in an era when Judeo-Christian ethics pervaded Western culture, they blanch at the idea of forsaking the "sacred hour" of eleven o'clock, Sunday morning. "I feel almost disloyal if I don't go *somewhere* Sunday morning," Claire, a fifty-eight-year-old English teacher, says of her ingrained habits. Yet she confesses to a nagging sense of restlessness with the traditional church.

Predictably, the farther you move down the age scale the less resistance you find to change, including the decision to leave the institutional church (IC) for other expressions of Christianity. Young Boomers, on the cusp of the Buster group, may straddle the fence for a while if they reach a point of spiritual inertia. Busters, and especially Mosaics, won't stick with anything for long if it doesn't ring true or relevant. In fact, writes Barna, "The great interest in spirituality among Baby Busters is assumed to have led them to embrace churches as their second home. Actually, Busters have the lowest level of church attendance, church giving, Sunday School involvement, small group participation, church volunteerism, Bible reading, discipleship involvement and use of Christian media. In short, in spite of their interest in spiritual matters, Busters are the single most disengaged population group in relation to organized religion."[6]

Little wonder then that alternative forms of "churching" appeal so much to the younger generations among us. And since youth culture plays the Pied Piper's tune that sets the standard for everyone else to follow, this trend away from traditionalism toward creative expressions of faith will likely only gain momentum in the next few years.

A young Boomer, Sheree claims that her spiritual journey in the IC mirrors the changes Western Christianity has gone through during the past three decades, from the freshness and purity of the early charismatic movement in the 1970s, to the "big church, big hair, big program" excesses of the '80s, to the quiet fallout and world-weariness of the '90s. A bedside prayer she spoke as a seven-year-old ushered her into the ranks of believers, and her family's religious background anchored that budding faith. "I grew up in a home where going to church was just what you did," she recalls. "When I got filled with the Spirit at age eighteen, I made the decision to become very involved in church. I grew closer to the Lord and steeped myself in the Word. It was the one experience in my life that felt like pure Christianity, and probably the closest to what a first-century church must have been like."

The midsize charismatic congregation she attended in Virginia was known for its solid teaching and family atmosphere. As a newlywed couple, Sheree and her husband joined a fellowship group where they basked in a sense of belonging and sang praise choruses taken right from the Psalms. "It felt like a true, bonded family. We would go there every Friday night—we couldn't wait for the weekend—because it was so fulfilling and deep," she says.

When the church's beloved pastor died, the flock dispersed, and Sheree found herself at a nearby megachurch where she joined the drama team and choir. "It was incredible to be part of a group of people who were so creative and in love with God," she says. For a few years the church remained vibrant and loving, but things started to sour after the leadership announced a massive new building program and later moved into a new three-thousand-seat auditorium. Sheree recalls watching the pastor strut across the stage bellowing out sermons like an enraged man. What she calls "the light-bulb moment" occurred one Sunday morning as she stood on a riser with the rest of the choir behind the church's stage curtain. It was only a few minutes to "show time," and she watched as the pastor barked a command to someone. "He was a little Hitler, but as soon as the curtain went up a whole new persona came out. It sickened me."

By 1989, dissension had infiltrated the church. "The more cocky he got, the worse it got," Sheree recalls. "I began to see a group of spiritual elite emerge—a spiritual clique, if you will. For example, the church had a prayer room, but only those who were more 'anointed' than others were allowed in. The sad thing is, some of the most 'elite' people were the worst ones to deal with one on one. When I got pregnant, my husband and I decided to move. My whole family was down in Florida, and I was sick of all this garbage going on at church. So we packed our belongings and moved south."

Once they settled in central Florida, Sheree and her husband started attending a large Pentecostal church. Trying to recapture a sense of belonging, she jumped into activities—sang in the choir, performed with a vocal ensemble, taught Sunday school, and worked a rotation in the nursery. Growing weary of the routine, she struggled to get out of bed and go to church. She eventually left and never went back.

The next church, an older evangelical denomination, provided a safe haven for Sheree for two or three years until the strain of a divorce and the death of her stepfather eroded the last threads of spiritual fervor she possessed. "Because I was once again very involved, and therefore high profile, the divorce came as a blow to a few people who didn't know the inside story well. One woman lashed out at me with a pious attitude. The choir director, a dear friend, hinted that I was backsliding. It wounded my spirit so bad my attendance started to slip. What they didn't realize was that my faith in God was still strong; I was just worn out and coming to the end of myself."

The Sunday after her stepfather's funeral, Sheree looked out from the choir loft at the sanctuary door where he always ushered—a door that now stood empty—and burst into tears. Unable to compose herself, she walked offstage. "I went back to church a couple more times and then just didn't have the energy or interest to go anymore," she says. "That was 1995. I tried visiting a few churches here and there, but I haven't attended a church regularly since then."

At the time of this interview, Sheree had found a Saturday night Bible study and looked forward to attending whenever her work schedule permitted. For now, that's how she defines church—and that definition is fine with her. As for the institutional church, she doesn't shut out the possibility of returning one day. "If I could find another New Covenant [her first church] I'd go in a heartbeat."

On the Shores of *Terra Nova*

Few arrive at the crossroads of IC departure without experiencing pangs of guilt and intensive self-interrogation. Sometimes it's other believers who give stern looks and shake their heads. Anyone at that crossroads can relate to the words of author Brian D. McLaren. Describing the thoughts that accompanied his burnout as a pastor and subsequent quest for a "new type of Christian," he writes:

> You can't talk about this sort of thing with just anybody. People worry about you. They may think you're changing sides, turning traitor. They may talk about you as if you came down with some communicable disease. So you keep this sort of thing like a dirty secret, this doubt that is not really a doubt about God or Jesus or faith but about our take on God, our version of Jesus, our way of faith. You let it out only when you feel you have found someone you can trust.
>
> And when you do, and the other person says, "I can't believe you're saying this. I have felt the same way, but I thought I was the only one"—that's a good moment. . . . And then, over time, the two of you discover you're not the only two, that there are many more out there . . . who are wrestling with the same discontent. . . . You begin to wonder if maybe you're at the

front edge of something—if your tentative and anxious steps "off the map" are actually the beginning of a new adventure in *terra nova,* new ground, fresh territory.[7]

That was the case for Laurie, whose childhood spiritual foundation led to a genuine personal hunger for more of God in her early twenties. While watching an evangelist on TV, she listened intently to the story of Christ dying for her sins, and tears started streaming down her face. "I thought, I want more of this," Laurie recalls. "That was the point I knew there was more, and I wanted to learn more. The Holy Spirit got introduced to me. The churches I had always attended didn't talk about the Holy Spirit; it was always God and Jesus, but not the Holy Spirit."

Laurie heard about a large Pentecostal church in her city and took a chance on it. From the first moment she walked in, she knew she'd found what she was searching for. "It was so alive it was electric," she says. "When they gave the altar call, I walked forward. We [Laurie and her mother] attended for six years. I was so hungry. We'd go every time the doors were open—Wednesday night, Sunday morning, Sunday night—and we drove forty-five minutes to get there."

Once Laurie started working at a Christian company in town, she no longer felt the need to drive to church so often. The close friendships she formed at work became a kind of small group; the tight circle of women prayed for each other, took part in each other's lives, and helped one another through good and bad. But it was at that Christian company that the first hint of disillusionment crept into her view of Christianity—namely because of individuals whose words and actions seemed at odds with the label "Christian."

"All this sort of tarnished my view of the whole Christian thing," Laurie says. "Not Christ, but Christians. It had nothing at all to do with how I felt about Jesus." Once her "honeymoon phase" at the church passed, she settled into a spiritual routine, but the excitement had left. On top of that, the church started a multimillion-dollar building program that became a financial strain for everyone involved. Curiously, Laurie claims she felt a distinct difference in the church when the congregation moved from the small sanctuary to the new one. Tired of the drive and the slump she had settled into, she stopped going.

Hungry for Community

A truant for a few years, Laurie admits that whenever she's away from church for any length of time, she gets "this hunger again, this desire to be involved with the fellowship again. All along, I wanted to be involved in a community, so we went back to the church I attended as a child."

The small Methodist church counted among its members people Laurie and her mother had known thirty years earlier, including her Girl Scout leader. "We felt a strong sense of spiritual community," Laurie says. "It was almost like coming home. They had a new sanctuary [the old one had burned down], and we fit in really well. We were there for about two years, and then it happened all over again. At this point I had gotten more involved than ever before—taught Sunday school, attended potluck dinners, did things for the Christmas cantata."

Laurie says the pastor's habit of talking over her head—"shaking your hand but looking over your shoulder at somebody else"—prompted her to want to leave, but a phone call from a godly friend curtailed her flight. Laurie's friend told her that the minister had accepted another pastorate and would be leaving soon. The incoming pastor "really knew the Lord," her friend said, and the rumor proved to be true. During an especially traumatic time, when Laurie's mother was admitted to the hospital, the church gathered around them in loving, tangible ways—calling to check on them, bringing food, sending cards and flowers, praying continually. "These were not phony Christians who raised their hands in church and then wouldn't speak to you when they passed you," she says.

The genuine outpouring of love and concern at the Methodist church sustained Laurie for a while, but eventually, she says, "We got bored with the church. The pastor was good, but the praise and worship was always dead. The organist played these dirges all the time, and the music was so depressing you'd leave there feeling down."

After trying out a few other local churches—no more long drives—Laurie and her mother stopped attending altogether. That was two years ago; they haven't been to church since.

Spiritually, Laurie's faith has never waned, she claims. "I feel closer to the Lord now than I ever have. My relationship with God never really changed. It's just church itself. I'm tired of it. I have my devotions, read the Bible every night, my mom and I pray together every night. None of that has changed. But the whole church scene, I'm just really turned off to it. I've watched myself go through the same pattern—up and down, up and down. It's happened for so many years. Right now, I have absolutely no desire to go to church."

Laurie doesn't rule out the possibility she may return to the IC someday. "It's a pattern. When I'm away from it for a while, I have that hunger and want to be back in it," she says. "Right now is not the time, but it will happen. I don't feel guilty about it either. Not going to church doesn't change how I feel about God or how he feels about me. If he convicts me to go somewhere, I will. There are people who go to church for all the wrong reasons. When I go, I want it to be for all the right reasons. Right now, I'm in the stage where I really don't care what happens to [the institutional] church."

Although in casual conversation she refers to "church" as a building where a group of believers meet, Laurie knows that's not what Jesus had in mind when he told Peter, "On this rock I will build My church, and the gates of Hades shall not prevail against it" (Matt. 16:18). So what is this thing called *church*?

4

WHAT IS THIS THING CALLED CHURCH?

The multicultural city, regarded as the commercial hub of the surrounding areas, attracted people eager for the sophistication and wealth that could be obtained from its busy port traffic. With its melting-pot population came the inevitable influx of diverse religions—some mystical, some pagan, some God-centered but layered with rules and regulations. Goddess worship abounded. Over time the city earned a reputation for its smorgasbord of religions, and a flourishing trade sprang up from the sale of religious articles. Like most big cities, sex and entertainment lured the eyes and excess cash of anybody willing to pay.

The city could be any large port in America today—San Francisco, Los Angeles, New York. But it went by a name that sounds strange on our postmodern tongues: Ephesus. As a strategic coastal gateway to the Eastern world, Ephesus grew to be the second largest city in the Roman Empire and one of the seven wonders of the ancient world. The hub of first-century Asia Minor, Ephesus was best known for its magnificent temple of Diana, where the worst kinds of sexual perversion (performed in the name of worship) took place. Vendors located outside the temple's doors sold instruments of magic and likenesses of the sensual goddess.

Enter a slight Jewish man with a potent personality.[1] Word of his towering intellect preceded him, but other educated men—especially those trained in Judaic law and the Scriptures—sparred verbally with him everywhere he went. They were not his primary goal, however. Instead, Paul focused his attention on the common people, ordinary citizens who found themselves trapped between the lure of their culture and the strange yet wonderful words that spilled from the apostle's mouth. Words of God. Words about a peculiar rabbi named Jesus who had died on a cross like so many other revolutionaries. Words about a new religion formed after the rabbi's death and—some whispered—bodily resurrection.

After a handful of Ephesians expressed faith in Christ, they started meeting together informally to hear Paul teach from the Scriptures, to pray, to share a meal, and sing psalms. A couple named Aquila and Priscilla hosted these gatherings in their home, and the believers—collectively called "the church"—started to build community with one another. Word of the good news spread, and friends brought other friends to the house meetings.

Though they didn't realize it at the time, the Romans unwittingly helped spread the gospel by building roads and creating shipping routes throughout the vast empire. Paul traveled by sea to Ephesus toward the end of his second missionary journey. He had already visited the city of Philippi, where the very first church was established on European soil in the home of Lydia, a successful businesswoman from Thyatira (see Acts 16:14–15). In his follow-up letters to believers in Rome, Corinth, and Colossae, Paul encouraged them to greet the churches that met in the homes of fellow believers (see Rom. 16:3-5; 1 Cor. 16:19; Col. 4:15).

House churches flourished throughout the latter first century and into the next two centuries as the gospel infiltrated the gentile world. Only when the Roman Emperor Constantine embraced Christianity and declared it the state religion did the church organize into a hierarchical institution. The new spiritual elite constructed massive cathedrals in key cities for believers to gather in. Smaller towns witnessed the expansion of church buildings—edifices that came to be known as "churches" rather than the people who gathered in them.

"We talk about the church building when we go to the church; they spoke of the congregation that met in someone's house," writes Calvin Guy in an article titled "Pilgrimage Toward the House Church: Controls That Limit the Spread of the Gospel." Guy, a former chairman of the Missions Department of Southern Baptist Theological Seminary, notes that the simplicity of the early church empowered it for missions and humanitarian aid. "Spared both the expense and concern of erecting and maintaining a building, they were soon involved in expending all available funds in loving service to the widows and orphans. Charity was not the incidental, fractional percentage of the budget. It was the budget."[2]

From the early Middle Ages until the twentieth century, the body of Christ continued to meet in buildings. Our identification with "church" became so attached to the idea of a physical structure that, long after believers splintered into denominations, we struggle to remember its original meaning. In the wake of spiritual burnout and churchianity, however, many believers have started to take a cue from countries like China, where persecution has driven the church underground (back into house gatherings)—as well as from Scripture itself. While many church denominations were witnessing their memberships slip over the past decade, a quiet grassroots revolution was sweeping North America.

"Yes, we are right now in the midst of the early days of a sovereign, very radical, move of God," says Nate Krupp, publisher of the book *God's Simple Plan for His Church*, on his website, titled Radical Christianity (www.radchr.net). "We are seeing God do incredible things: people are leaving the IC by the thousands; they are tired of being an audience, instead of a body; they question increasingly all the money that goes into buildings; they are tired of being controlled and manipulated; they long to use their giftings to serve God and see 'the priesthood of all believers,' instead of 'the clergy,' and they long to see the Holy Spirit allowed to freely move instead of everything being controlled. God is sovereignly, in these days, raising up a massive, growing movement of people who are desiring to function like the early Christians in the Book of Acts. Believers are turning their backs on all the programs and returning to their first love, Jesus."

A Winter's Revelation

As a young evangelist in the 1960s, Krupp traveled throughout North America training believers how to share their faith. He'd work with congregations for two weeks at a time, spending long hours teaching the people how to talk about Jesus in the real world. "We'd see marvelous things happen, and there would always be a core of people who wanted to continue evangelizing," Krupp says. Six months later he'd call to see how things were going. Over the years a pattern emerged from the churches. During his checkup calls, the pastors would tell him they no longer held the evangelism outreaches, what with choir practice and home groups and potluck suppers eating up the church week.

Frustrated that his efforts bore so little lasting fruit, Krupp asked God what was up. He sensed the Lord telling him there would be no New Testament evangelism until there were

New Testament Christians, and no New Testament Christians until there were New Testament churches. But what, really, did a New Testament church look like?

In the winter of 1966 Krupp traveled to a small town in upstate New York for yet another evangelism conference. A blizzard bore down on the region, and no one could get through. Forced to cancel the conference—and trapped by three feet of snow—Krupp and the pastor of the church hunkered down to wait out the storm. "I discovered that the pastor and I were both seeking answers from the Lord: Does he have an answer for his church, and if he does, what is that answer? We spent a whole week fasting and praying for answers. The conclusions we came to after that week were so radical we didn't know what to do with it."

Krupp came away from the weeklong Bible study convinced that Western believers were going about church all wrong. Instead, he says, God was calling his people back to the radical Christianity of the New Testament. Two decades later, in 1987, Krupp sensed God telling him, "Now is the time." As a result of those four words he became a home-based-church evangelist of sorts, traveling the globe with the message. Krupp characterizes radical Christianity as a move away from clergy-dominated services to informal gatherings of believers, with an emphasis on servant leadership.

"Everywhere I went I detected a restlessness in God's people," he says. "People were just dissatisfied, tired of going and sitting, tired of the control, tired of everything being done up on the platform, tired of being a nonfunctioning part of the body. A lot of people didn't even know why they were restless; they just knew something was not right."

These days Krupp and his wife no longer travel but maintain their ministry via their website. "I get inquiries from all over the world. [This spiritual awakening] is happening everywhere," Krupp says. "Hardly a week goes by that I don't hear from somebody."

The Clergy-Laity Divide

Nineteenth-century church historian Philip Schaff dates the splitting of believers into clergy and laity to the third century, when the term *priest* was applied to Christians with leadership gifts, especially bishops. "In the same manner the whole ministry, and it alone, was called 'clergy,' with a double reference to its presidency and its peculiar relation to God. . . . In the apostolic church preaching and teaching were not confined to a particular class, but every convert could proclaim the gospel to unbelievers, and every Christian who had the gift could pray and teach and exhort in the congregation. The New Testament knows no spiritual aristocracy of nobility, but calls all believers 'saints' though many fall far short of their vocation," Schaff writes.[3]

Depending on whom you ask, the grassroots movement toward informal gatherings as "church" is alternately labeled healthy and dangerous. Krupp says most believers he encounters warm to the idea of starting home-based churches. Clergy are another story. "Except for the few that God opens the eyes of, the clergy are skeptical at best and antagonistic at worst. The average believer is more open to what God is saying and doing. Of course [a pastor] has a lot more at stake—his job, his retirement, his home, his identity, his everything."

The Sanhedrin stoned Stephen, the first Christian martyr, for his shocking rebuke that "the Most High does not dwell in temples made with hands" (Acts 7:48). According to New Testament theologians, the Temple—and the livelihood of the priests that was tied to it—was such a vital component of Jewish worship and identity that detractors like Stephen literally placed their lives on the line.

Believers who choose to leave the IC today may be called spiritual renegades—even cultic—yet no one labels the New Testament Christians rebels. Despite the verbal assaults, twenty-first-century believers are leaving the organized church in droves. Some families meet together to practice their faith while others network with house churches in their area or create spontaneous gatherings. "The movement is so large I don't even try to keep up with it," Krupp says. "Just look at the number of home church websites on the Internet. It's phenomenal."[4]

He asserts that the home-church movement is characterized by fourteen traits:

- from serving God to knowing God
- from a gospel of "easy-believism" to the gospel of the kingdom
- from the efforts of man to the works of God
- from insecure, wounded people to people made whole by Jesus Christ
- from being told by man what to do to learning to hear God's voice and doing what he tells you to do
- from clergy-dominated services and programs to mutually participating communities of believers
- from one-man leadership to team, servant leadership
- from being meeting-oriented to being relationship-oriented
- from gathering in church buildings to gathering in homes
- from looking inward to looking outward
- from big, expensive programs of evangelism to the simple, Spirit-led witness of "the little people"
- from the subjugation of women to a release of women as equal partners in the kingdom of God
- from financial sloppiness and cover-up to financial integrity, accountability, and disclosure
- from denominations to "the church of a city"

Frying-Pan Faith

Any new experience wears the sheen of "newness" and seems impervious to tarnish. It's no wonder then that believers bailing out of the IC greet the house church with high expectations and stars in their eyes. Yet, being human, we take our problems with us—no matter where we go.

In her article "Help! My House Church Is Worse Than the Institutional Church Ever Was!" Tracey Amino writes, "Just because we leave the IC doesn't mean that we are magically cleaned up. The only thing that really changes immediately is that we are free from the bondage of hierarchy. However, all of the problems that, in many cases, were dormant inside of us while we were in the IC (because we didn't know anyone well enough for them to detect, or no one saw them, or for whatever reason) are still there when we leave the IC. So, looking at things in the natural, the situation can appear to be even worse than the IC sometimes—especially when people's weaknesses are exposed and we try to move forward being relational and allowing the Lord to bring us to maturity."[5]

Amino likens a believer new to the house-church setting to a child adopted into a family from an orphanage. At first, the child has trouble transitioning into a relational family environment. Years of institutionalization have to be "unlearned" before the child trusts enough to be herself around the new family members. "Does that mean that you're a failure and that the child would be better off back in the orphanage?" Amino asks. "No, it just means that it's going to take some work on your part to help the child make the transition from an institutionalized lifestyle to a familial [or relational] one."[6]

She's not the only one who embraces this organic style of "churching" and yet sees its imperfections all too clearly. In his tongue-in-cheek article "My Gripes about the House Church Movement," writer Andrew Jones asserts:

The label needs to change from house church to something that better describes it. The house church network in Prague started 6 months ago. People meet in many different venues but none meet in a house. People there cannot afford a house. "Home church" is better, but they don't always meet in homes. Clubs? Yes. Dunkin' Donuts? Yes. Apartments? Sometimes. Neil Cole called them Simple Churches. I like that. Organic Church. Micro Church. . . .

Somebody, somewhere, needs to give people a little slack. Some space to be pluralistic. Someone needs to integrate the new history and the new structure with the previous generation of churches. To stand on their shoulders rather than slap their cheeks. The Holy Spirit utilized the old-school Festival of Pentecost to kick off something new. The disciples launched out from the Temple. Paul started in synagogues. Why can't the house church leaders be players in the wider picture of what God is doing among the old AND new wineskins? . . .

Let's all just get along. Let's be honest about where we are in this transition. Let's not spill any wine. Let's not spoil the fun of pastors surfing the previous wave. Let's preserve the old wineskins and birth the new ones.[7]

Krupp admits that, like any new movement born of God, the home-based-church movement can get off track. It can be taken over and controlled by man, or it can continue to develop into all that God intends, he says. "When man takes over, and men begin to control men, the Holy Spirit is grieved, and we are left with just a human organization. This has happened often in the past, leaving us with today's denominations."[8]

He's identified ten steps that lead down the "slippery slope" toward organized religion and cautions worshippers not to fall into the trap. Those steps are: incorporating, having a name, having a statement of faith, owning property, using titles, offering salaries, using the term *house church,* networking, supporting trans-local ministries, and exhibiting a we-they mentality.

Using the term *house church*? Networking? How can those things possibly be detrimental, we wonder. Krupp offers an explanation for his rationale:

> There are currently at least three types of "new wine skins" developing around the world. They use the descriptive terms of open church, cell church, and house church. Anyone familiar with what God is doing today knows what each of these terms means. This can be a good thing in helping to communicate the particular type of group that may exist. But the use of these terms can also have an excluding effect. You may feel that you are part of the "cell church movement" and therefore not a part of the "house church movement." We must continue to see ourselves as simply part of the Body of Christ. We would do well to not use terms that divide, but just say something like, "We are a group of believers in Jesus, who meet from house to house."[9]

His worries about networking stem from the all-too-human tendency to clan together. "Once several similar home groups develop in a given area, and discover one another, they usually want to get together occasionally," Krupp says. "This networking, built on relationships, can be a very healthy function. But if this network of groups takes on a name . . . it is a big step toward denominationalism. If the networking becomes a we-they network, it also is a big step toward denominationalism. We must learn how to network and co-labor without denominating."[10]

Jackie, a single mother of two, started a Saturday night Bible study with a handful of friends because she gave up on trying to find a church that fit—or one that didn't remind her of the last two churches she attended, where subtle abuses crept in over a period of months or years.

"We're still in the baby stage—we've only been meeting for a few weeks—but so far it's what I've been looking for," she says. "All of us were starved for authentic community, and we also shared a hunger to dig into the Word, so that's what we're doing. I imagine we'll get on each other's nerves from time to time. It's unrealistic to expect perfection; but collectively we were all just so tired of the institutional church."

A Changing Landscape

Krupp believes the spiritual landscape of North America is ripe for the expansion of house churches. "If you believe the Bible teaches a period of intense persecution of believers at the end of this age, it would be easy to see that what's happened in China could well happen here," he states. "Other things could also force the church into homes—an energy crisis, economic collapse, political upheaval. I believe before Jesus returns the true church will be meeting in homes, and I definitely think we're at the end of the age. It could all be wrapped up in the next twenty-five years."

Few doubt that something wonderful is stirring the landscape. Whenever God starts moving behind the scenes, the spiritual receptors of his people begin to pick up the same signal at the same time. "A radical conversation has been quietly taking place in coffee shops and living rooms, during small events and at not-well-publicized conferences, in person and online," Brian McLaren, author of *A New Kind of Christian,* states on the www.emergentvillage.com website. "It involves thousands of people from countries all over the world. It's about Christian faith, life, thought, and ministry in the emerging postmodern culture."

Whatever expressions that "radical conversation" takes, legitimate questions and concerns surface among those with a vested interest in the future life and health of the church. Will the new forms of "church" provide a structure or environment that nurtures the growth of godly leadership? What about the sacraments? Will these looser forms of organic fellowship follow Christ's own dictates for what the church should be? Will new believers be adequately discipled? Finally, although informal gatherings for "God talk" abound, what are these people really gathering around? In the end we have to trust the future of the church to Christ and do our best to be faithful stewards of the heavenly gifts.

Perhaps the best of both worlds—preserving the old wineskins while making room for the new—will emerge as the twenty-first-century model church historians someday write about us. What those new wineskins will look like, of course, is the burning question in emerging church leaders' minds.

One thing is for sure: True to the nature of our media-savvy culture, the emerging church is not confined to the dimensions of time and place—or to the physical structure of a building or house. By the millions, people are finding God and spiritual community in alternative ways, including online.

5

From Religion 101 to Spirituality.com

When cell phones first hit the market, an interstate billboard in my city boldly declared, "Someday you'll wonder how you ever got along without one." The ad showed a cellular phone from a now-prominent vendor. *Right,* I thought. But the ad proved true. Ditto for the Internet. In the mid-1990s, when I first read about some bizarre new medium called the "Information Superhighway," or Internet, I dismissed it as the domain of tech-heads. Definitely not something I would be cueing into. "One day Americans will conduct most of their research, send mail, and even shop via the Internet," technology analysts predicted. The statement seemed as far-fetched as the mid-1970s assertion that within thirty years people would live on the moon. But not only did all those predictions come true (except the part about the moon), they happened a lot sooner than some prognosticators imagined.

I had a similar reaction when demographer George Barna predicted that by the early twenty-first century many Americans would trade in their church sanctuaries for cyber-churches, getting their spiritual needs met (including community) online. Eating crow has become a regular pastime for me.

In their book *Boiling Point,* Barna and coauthor Mark Hatch wrote:

> The biggest area of growth in religious activity will be in people turning to the Internet for religious information and experiences. Already, 1 out of every 10 adults (and an even higher percentage of teenagers) use the Net for religious purposes. That will jump to about 1 out of 4 adults by the close of this decade in response to greater Net penetration, usage of the Net for a broader range of life needs and interests, the aging of the two digital generations, the explosion of Net-oriented products that will appear and the increased reliance on the Net as a communication vehicle by churches. However, many who use the Internet for religious endeavors will engage in nontraditional pursuits such as holding theological discussions, participating in real-time worship, joining with others from around the world in real-time prayer and taking religious courses on-line. For some people, the Internet will supplement what they receive from their local church; for millions of others, the Internet will replace it.[1]

For hundreds of thousands of Western believers, "church" is indeed now a cyber-community they've created on sites such as Beliefnet.com, virtualchurch.org, christiansnet.com, or cyber-church.com. As one web page on geocities.com states, "A cyberchurch facilitates worship and Christian education, evangelization and community on the World Wide Web. . . . A cyberchurch is above all, *interactive.* It communicates with people and aims to establish a relationship with the visitors."

If you browse any of these sites for a week or two, you'll quickly realize the same people log on day after day—or, more likely, night after night. With the workday behind them, many spiritual seekers spend the evening in front of their computer monitors chatting with other believers, reading online devotions and articles, or posting questions to electronic bulletin boards (and of course checking back frequently for responses). Topics of discussion range from gritty realism—"Will God punish me if I have sex with my boyfriend?"—to esoteric ruminations on the meaning of sanctification. Regular browsers in a cyber-community get to know other regulars by their usernames and frequently bare their souls to each other.

Barna was dead-on when he said (in 1998) that our culture has shifted away from viewing congregations as "church homes" to "spiritual pit stops," a trend that would pave the way for spiritual transience—and a pervasive sense of loneliness that sends us looking for community wherever we can find it, even if it's on the Web.

"Our inability to cultivate lasting communities of faith is partly a result of changes we have made to the church infrastructure, and partly a result of changing perspectives that people embrace toward their faith experience," he states. "More and more Americans are beginning to view churches as a 'rest stop' along their spiritual journey, rather than as their final destination." He notes that the rest-stop mentality is fueled by four main factors: our transience (15 to 20 percent of households relocate each year); our preference for variety; our perception that spiritual enlightenment comes from a discovery process rather than commitment to a faith group; and our approach to religion as a commodity we consume rather than something in which we invest ourselves.[2]

Regardless of how we feel about this spiritual transition, the reality is that people are hungry for God, and if they can fill that void by connecting with other believers online, they'll do it. In fact, that's just what many IC-weary believers are doing.

Online Seekers

Dean "walked away from the church—and God, or so I thought" about twenty years ago because (1) he equated being a Christian with fundamentalism and (2) "some of what I had been taught as a child and in Bible college didn't line up with what I saw in the Scriptures." Depressed, he drifted from place to place for several years and "learned how to make short-term friends," he says. About four years ago he started reading the Bible again and became re-convinced about Jesus. "Then I got my first computer, found Beliefnet, and this has been something like my church ever since." Dean attended one church for a few months but stopped going because the preaching seemed too fire-and-brimstone. On a positive note, he adds: "I'm beginning to feel that going back to church [someday] may be much more beneficial than I now realize, both for myself and the others there."

His story resonates with that of Lindsay, who also logs online to connect with other believers. After a traditional Lutheran upbringing, she became "semi-conscious of a need for a Savior" in her early twenties and accepted Christ but continued living life her way, she says. An encounter with a group of nontraditional Christians who "love Jesus and the Bible but were very anti–traditional church" prompted her to begin a journey of spiritual growth. Through her own biblical studies, a lot of prayer, and communication with her Christian friends she entered a phase of deep soul-searching.

"As of today, I am not connected to any particular church, though I am not averse to it," Lindsay says. "I only want to go where the Holy Spirit is and where he directs me. My husband and I spend daily time in prayer together and in reading the Bible and other Christian books. I believe a real shaking up of the whole church is necessary to bring the real church to a deep awakening. At the moment the 'institutional church' seems more like a humanistic club to me than a real godly spiritual body of Christ, which it is meant to be."

In her book *Give Me That Online Religion,* religion/philosophy professor Brenda Brasher likens the cyber-spirituality movement to a tidal wave, with ramifications typical of those that follow a tsunami:

> Some people already navigate the virtual world with grace and ease; others are hard at work constructing their first virtual surfboard. Whether you choose to surf or run, the tidal wave of computer-inspired spiritual change is coming. . . . Rushing toward us, online religion crashes against the shoals of more traditional religious ideas and practice. Sometimes it is pushed back by the encounter, but like the tidal wave it is, sometimes it overwhelms them—and anything else in its path.
>
> As cyberspace swiftly overtakes us, we can no longer choose to avoid the change it brings. Instead we must determine how best to respond. Given that outrunning a tidal wave is never an option, the best possibility open to us may be to run *toward* the wave, to leap into its force and surf its energies to a new shore.[3]

Away and Back Again

An active member of the Beliefnet Christian community (the site welcomes conversation on various religions), Rebecca spent several years away from organized Christianity and even opted out of Christianity altogether for a while. "Several factors contributed to what I like to call my thirty-something religious tantrum," she notes. "I had been a Lutheran all my life and a happy, enthusiastic, and involved layperson since my college days. Then I got a new job in a new community, and when I went to the local Lutheran congregation I was practically shunned as if I were a Pod Person. I'd sit in a pew; the other people in the pew would all move way over. No one introduced themselves to me. It was a very disillusioning slap in the face for someone who heretofore had nothing but positive church experiences as an adult."

Some friends at work invited Rebecca to worship with them at another local church. Things sailed along pretty well until a feud split the congregation. "It was as if the congregation were imploding," she says. At the same time, she became disillusioned by the "Falwell/Robertson style of American pop Christianity."

"Even though I was in a progressive congregation in a progressive denomination, I felt as if Christianity were being steamrollered by this reactionary movement," Rebecca says. "I thought, Well, if this is the direction organized Christianity is headed, the heck with it . . . so I dropped out."

Rebecca says that what brought her back to Christianity and to a faith community was the grace of God—in the form of an intense longing for the Eucharist. She visited a small country church where she discovered, to her delight, her former college campus pastor installed. "The moment I walked in the building, I felt 'home' in a very intense way. Receiving Communion that day was like a starving, thirsty refugee finally reaching food and drink. The people in this church were also friendly and welcoming right from the get-go. Anyhow, that is what drove me away from organized religion and what drew me back."

As another cyber-spirituality browser wrote, "God does not want any of us to settle for secondhand religion; he wants us to have a real experience with him. Sometimes that is done in community and often it is done on the 'mountain' alone with just him."

Whether we connect with other believers online or in person, our very *humanness* all too easily muddies the spiritual waters that once looked so bright and clear. In the next chapter we'll explore what happens when community turns into performance and "working" for God takes precedence over knowing him.

6

WORKING HARD AT BEING GOOD

Nobody worked harder for the church than Beatrice. If a Sunday school class needed teaching, she'd teach it. If the nursery needed a supervisor, she'd step up to the plate. "The more I did the closer I got to God, or so I was taught," Beatrice says. "My problem was that I didn't feel like I was getting closer to God. I was very unhappy, bored, and just plain tired."

An experience at the altar changed her thinking. In the church service one evening, she felt heaviness in her heart. The day had been difficult, and she was weary—weary of her job, weary of the need to do the good deeds set before her, weary of all the things that dragged her down to a low ebb. For weeks she had been anything but uplifted in the midweek services that were supposed to help get her through the week.

In the midst of her thoughts, she became aware of what the musician was playing on the keyboard: "Sitting at his feet, sitting at his feet." The words painted a stark contrast to her hectic life. "I immediately headed for the altar and poured my heart out to the Lord," Beatrice says. "I sobbed quietly, and then I sensed the Lord saying to me, 'Be a Mary; no more Martha.' "

She mentally told God how busy she was—she couldn't possibly relinquish her many duties: kitchen patrol, choir, childbirth classes, Sunday school class. "I SAID, NO MORE MARTHA," the impression came again, this time more insistently.

"It was as though he were saying, 'Read my lips,' " Beatrice quips. "But how could I give up all those works? These areas were important to me. I've always been busy in church. The jobs no one wanted I would do. If they needed door prizes for a party, I made them. Clean the kitchen? There I was with my mop and broom. Food for the grieving? My casserole dish was full. I got up from that altar a different person. I was truly willing to do what he asked, but it was a struggle to let go of all these things."

Beatrice said that over the years her life had come to resemble her mother's apron pockets. "All my mother's aprons had a big pocket, and as she cleaned house she would pick up bits and pieces—a safety pin, a paper clip, a penny, an odd button, a bobby pin or two," she says. "Soon that pocket would be overflowing with junk. Wasn't my life like that? My *spiritual apron* had a pocketful of junk."

At the altar that night she cut the apron strings. The next time someone asked her to do a job at church, she said no. For weeks she gradually dropped a meeting here, a function there. One night, she looked into the Word and read in Luke 10:38–42:

Now it happened as they went that He entered a certain village; and a certain woman named Martha welcomed

Him into her house. And she had a sister called Mary, who also sat at Jesus' feet and heard His word. But Martha was distracted with much serving, and she approached Him and said, "Lord, do You not care that my sister has left me to serve alone? Therefore tell her to help me." And Jesus answered and said to her, "Martha, Martha, you are worried and troubled about many things. But one thing is needed, and Mary has chosen that good part, which will not be taken away from her."

"I desperately wanted to do his will," Beatrice says. "The only way I would don that apron again is if he filled the pocket with *joy, love, grace, peace, and faith*. Things that can be shared with others. I wanted to be the Mary he wanted me to be."

Again and again she pondered the things God had taught her. She dug into the Word and studied his miracles. She looked for things to do that would benefit the kingdom of God rather than her own sense of purpose. God led Beatrice onto a new path of service that was so much more rewarding than the treadmill of works that carried her along for so many years, she says. But God had even more in store for her.

Eventually Beatrice and her husband were invited to a small fellowship meeting their son attended. "That first night I sat on the floor with my car keys in my hands, ready to run for the front door if they said anything I didn't agree with," she says. "Nothing was said to that effect. In fact, the love that was shown us was something I had never experienced in my many years of churchgoing. We kept going back every Thursday night."

Unhappy in her "regular" church, Beatrice says the Wednesday night services were so predictable she got bored. "I knew exactly what would be said, who would testify, what songs would be sung, and how the service would end. Especially the part where we had to go to the altar or be accused of having sin in our life."

After two years in the fellowship meetings, Beatrice and her husband finally walked away from their denominational church. "We went from thirty-five years of guilt and condemnation to six years of freedom and rest in Jesus," she says. "I've sent letters to friends and relatives and asked their forgiveness for my self-righteousness. I wrote my former boss and asked her to forgive me for being such a religious snob. I was the best fruit [of the Spirit] inspector around, and I was proud of it. How Christ must have wept over my wrong thinking. Now each day is filled with his joy and peace and rest."

Toxic Roles

In the conversations that led to this book, again and again believers—especially those who have been in church most or all of their lives—said they are just plain tired. Tired of serving. Tired of "doing good." Tired of the spiritual treadmill that so often accompanies participation in a local church. The 80/20 rule abounds in congregations as surely as it does in corporate hallways. When that hardworking 20 percent (who do 80 percent of the work, as the formula goes) hit the wall regarding service, they often end up spiritually, emotionally, and physically fatigued. No wonder the New Testament model for church describes a functioning body in which *all* the members contribute to the whole. When the burden of a community's spiritual needs is piled on the shoulders of one person, or even on a select few in leadership, you can be sure those individuals will eventually stagger under the weight of it.

Jon Zens, editor of the quarterly publication *Searching Together*, describes what the current one-person model of church leadership often translates into: "While the traditional one-man, church building model has some visible success, there are many undeniable statistics that point to the reality of such success being short term. Divorce, suicide, nervous breakdown, burnout, etc., abound among clergy. The average pastorate in the Southern Baptist Convention is under 18 months. The high-pressure altar call tactics have proven to produce 'converts' that rarely last. Even with all the empirical evidence that many things are amuck in the traditional model, the real issue is 'What does the NT teach?' If any model contradicts or stifles the New Testament pattern, it should be jettisoned for such reasons alone. The early church had no clergy and no sacred buildings, and in this regard was radically different from all other religions, including Judaism. The proliferation of expensive church buildings constitutes a fundamental compromise of what Christ intended to build. Thus, believers gathering in informal settings [in] homes, rented store-fronts, outdoors and apartments apparently provides the best context for the 58 'one anothers' [in the Bible] to be fleshed out."[1]

For those in church leadership, "doing" ministry is part-and-parcel of their job description, or so the current church model renders it. But for others, like Beatrice, doing good works "for the Lord" may be a subconscious cry for approval—from God and others. In their book *Toxic Faith,* Stephen Arterburn and Jack Felton describe a "toxic role" often played out by believers who yearn for acceptance but mistakenly replace godly dependency with self-reliance. For those caught in a "works" treadmill, spiritual fervor has morphed into religious addiction.

These people "have found in their faith and religion a place where they can obtain what they always wanted and needed: acceptance, a way to be valued and esteemed," Arterburn and Felton write. "They find security and hope in a growing trust in God. However, when they no longer focus on God, their faith becomes toxic. Then everything is done for self in the name of God rather than every possible sacrifice of self being made in the name of God. This happens because the focus on God shifts to self and also to the fruit of the relationship with God. . . . The sinful self-obsession leads

71

to idolatry and worship of those feelings that are developed through faith. Searching for the feelings, not God, becomes an addictive obsession. The feelings were not bad, but they soured when they became the sole motivation for the relationship with God."[2]

Sometimes, as in the case of our next story, the pressure to perform (or carry a heavy load) is placed upon believers by a "toxic faith system"—a church body that thrives on the participation of religious addicts. Requested to "serve, serve, and serve some more," the members of the group sacrifice their time, their abilities, and even their families for the good of the community—or so they are told. "This level of service often becomes overwhelming," state Arterburn and Felton. "People become so drained that they can't think clearly. Their emotions become distorted. Deep depression, extreme anxiety, and a general numbness are common in overwhelmed religious addicts. Activity takes precedence and dries the soul of the addicts, leaving many feeling hopeless and some the victims of total breakdown. Leaders in the system wonder why so many become involved but then fall away from the faith. They are burned out by the service demands of the system."[3]

Beautiful Beginnings

For four weeks in a row, Glen had invited Marcia to attend some Jesus Freak meeting with him, and for four weeks in a row she had turned him down. She still couldn't get over the change in this once-cool guy who had partied with her and other college students in the rooming house where they all lived. After Glen got religion, one by one he infected the other tenants with his Jesus virus, and they now spent their Friday nights talking about God and playing harps, for all Marcia knew. One thing she did know was that she wanted no part of this Jesus stuff that was spreading like an epidemic back in 1972; she went so far as to move out of the rooming house to avoid the Jesus germ.

Jesus. The name was familiar to Marcia. Like many Baby Boomers, she had grown up in the church, but the electricity of the counterculture movement proved too strong to resist, and the religion of her mother smacked of the Establishment—definitely a thing to be rejected. "I wanted nothing to do with the God they preached, a deity that struck me as a cross between a cosmic bouncer and a circuit-court judge," Marcia says.

But God wasn't that easy to dismiss, Marcia discovered. As she crammed for finals, nagging spiritual thoughts crawled through her mind. Months earlier, another friend had introduced her to satanism and witchcraft, and by all accounts, they offered a kind of power that really worked. If anybody needed power, she did. Maybe the right kind of power could wipe out all the garbage in her life and make her forget those memories that still stalked her night and day—memories of things she swore she would never do but did anyway. So she flirted with satanism, but meanwhile she had Glen and Jesus to contend with. The change in Glen's life was undeniable. And the freakiest thing happened to his eyes. They were the same soft blue they'd always been, but now they radiated *something*.

When the fifth Friday rolled around, Marcia braced herself for yet another phone call from Glen, but it never came. Wasn't he going to invite her to the meeting? Or had her streak of refusals quenched his enthusiasm? As the afternoon wore on, something—God? the power of reverse psychology?—propelled her into action. She called Glen—and caught him just as he was leaving for the meeting. She invited herself along and immediately regretted it.

The living room of the oceanfront house where the meeting was held was packed with college students. The speaker that night was a professor who had arrived on a motorcycle; she dismissed him as a phony like everyone else in the room.

Now in a decidedly foul mood, Marcia tuned him out. "To this day I don't recall anything else he said that night, but one thing burned itself into my memory," she says. "He said these exact words: 'God not only forgave your sins, he forgot them.'"

And to this day, Marcia has no idea why she suddenly believed those words. She turned to her friend Chris, who was sitting on the floor next to her. "I whispered to Chris that we needed to talk. He led me out to the front porch where we could be alone, and there, without a word, I experienced the very real love and forgiveness of God."

Into the Sheepfold

The old Marcia changed virtually overnight into someone her friends didn't recognize—someone she certainly didn't recognize. Instead of spending every night in a bar, she bought a Bible and spent her evenings alone in her room, reading and studying.

At the Friday night meetings, Marcia encountered what she believed the first-century church must have been like. The contrast with what she experienced in typical church services was unsettling, so when a "New Testament" church started up in her area, she was there from the very beginning. It didn't take long for the church to move away from New Testament principles, but Marcia turned a blind eye. "My job was to serve God through the church and support the leaders even when I disagreed with their actions," she says. "I kept my mouth shut, but my heart was slowly breaking. For eleven long years I stayed, convinced I was pleasing God by remaining faithful to the church even as I watched my beloved congregation turn into a country club."

Most of her friends left the fellowship within a few years after it started. They warned Marcia (now married) that she would become a "Stepford wife"—a mindlessly obedient servant who looked right, acted right, and said all the right things. Deep down, she knew they were right. The Sunday morning services were well-honed performances. "Put on a good show and the masses will come. That was the apparent thinking," Marcia says. "Church members were expected—actually, required—to dress a certain way and show up for every service, class, meeting, or other event. Dressing 'a certain way' meant wearing the most expensive clothes you could. The leadership wanted to attract wealthier members, so we had to look as if we had money too. This was not a subtle, disguised message; it was stated clearly in ministry meetings I attended as head of the nursery."

Everyone tithed, of course. Marcia had heard stories of what happened to members who didn't, though she found those stories hard to believe—that is, until her own family hit on hard times. One week she wrote out a check for the entire balance in their checking account, $68.73. "That was all the money we had in the world, and I believed God had directed me to give it to the church," Marcia recalls. "The following week, the pastor pointed out from the pulpit how petty people can be with their money. 'We're so precise with our tithes that we quibble over pennies, writing out checks for ridiculous amounts like $68.73—we wouldn't dare give God a penny over our tithe!' he said, assuming my check represented a tithe on $687.30. I wish that had been the case. Although I had tithed for eight years at that point, he believed I had suddenly turned stingy with God—and with him. I cried once I got alone, but I eventually let it go."

Another situation should have sent Marcia running for the door, she says, but still she hung in there. One of the musicians was married to an unbeliever. The congregation prayed for him to become a believer, and eventually he did. The leadership gave him a prominent position in the still-small fellowship. "I felt uneasy in my spirit and decided to talk to the pastor's wife about it," Marcia says. "'Are you sure he's ready for that kind of—' I started to ask. She put her hand up in front of my face. The unmistakable message: Never question a leadership decision. *Run along, little girl, and let the big boys handle this.*" The big boys, however, had botched up. The star convert had been having an affair with his secretary for years, and once he was found out, he refused to give her up and divorced his wife.

A few years later, a similar incident occurred. "I watched as other shocking incidents piled up at this church, yet I stayed, leaving only when an out-of-state move forced me to," Marcia says. "Not until I got away from that church did I realize the damage it had wrought on me. I had lost touch with who I was and who God wanted me to be. I had sacrificed my family to the altar of church; we were still together, but I had a lot of bad religious habits to unlearn. Worst of all, I had substituted church for God. I hardly knew him anymore. I had been so caught up in serving the church that I failed to maintain an intimate relationship with Jesus."

Marcia has attended other churches since then and even joined one. But every time she thinks she's found a church that's different, she says, "I hold my breath, keep my hopes in check, and give it a try—for years. Meanwhile, my spirit cries out to God for some sign that we'll eventually stop playing church."

She finally walked away from the institutional church after nearly thirty years of watching one church after another put on a show for God—or rather, for man. Her miserable spiritual state, compounded by a genetic tendency toward melancholy, spiraled her into a black depression. Overwhelmed by heavy responsibilities at a new job, she sank even deeper into the pit. "The worst thing about it was that, instinctively, I knew Christians are not supposed to be depressed," Marcia says. "So I put a tight clamp on my secret and smiled bravely at the world."

WORKING HARD AT BEING GOOD

Permission to Seek

Most people's lives, if viewed as the screen of a heart monitor, would appear like a straight line with occasional blips in it. The blips vary in frequency and intensity depending on what's going on in our lives. Some represent highs, others lows. They may seem insignificant at the time, but when seen through the lens of hindsight, some events take on huge proportions, becoming the high-water marks of our life stories.

For Marcia, one of those seemingly insignificant "blips" occurred as she listened to an audio book by a one-time Christian television celebrity who had battled depression. "The account of her experience assured me it was not a sin to go on antidepressant medication," Marcia says. "In that moment, it was as if God himself acknowledged my illness and gave me permission to seek medical help so I could get to a point where I could hear his voice again. I had sunk so low I could not even sense his presence in my life until the medication pulled me out of the pit I was in."

No Damascus Road light knocked Marcia off her feet, but God had walked out to meet her in the wilderness. She recognized him another Sunday morning when she attended a small service conducted by a low-key, itinerant ministry. Afterward, she met one of the pastors.

"As I stood there talking to him, I was jarred by the awareness that he never took his eyes off me," Marcia says. "He never looked around for someone more important to talk to. He looked me straight in the eye and listened to every word I said. As we shook hands and turned away from each other, tears welled up in my eyes. For the first time in thirty years, a pastor had *listened* to me. He wanted to hear what was in my heart. He didn't look over my head to find a more influential person to greet. He gave me hope.

"Will I return to church someday? Probably. Christians are hopelessly hopeful. We try to ward off cynicism, but then we go and set ourselves up for yet another disappointment. For me, that's okay. I'd rather remain vulnerable than not. In the meantime I have a higher priority, and that's returning to my first love—Jesus." Since the time Marcia told me her story, she has discovered Christ-centered worship in the liturgy of the Episcopal Church.

Spiritual Sinkholes

The stories of David, Jeremiah, and other prominent Bible heroes paint a stark contrast between the upbeat, always-joyful attitude we've somehow come to expect of believers and what most of us experience at one time or another in our own spiritual journeys. These spiritual sinkholes, or what John Bunyan in *The Pilgrim's Progress* called the "Slough of Despond," are an integral part of going deeper with God. In fact, it could be argued, they're necessary. As odd as it sounds, they're also the next best place to be on the spiritual road map to wholeness and rest. Authors Thomas Whiteman and Randy Petersen allude to this in their discussion of recovery from addictions:

> Depression stinks, but it's also the best place to be so far—because it's closer to acceptance. We don't want to be corny, but it's the darkness before the dawn. Only by staring at the awful face of the problem can you learn how to defeat it. . . .
>
> The [depressed person] has two directions from which to choose, up the mountain or down it, through the process or backward. It's easy to go back down the mountain, but that will just make the climb tougher. . . . Seldom does anyone go through all the stages in order; there is regular slippage. But eventually progress occurs, and the person reaches the cave of depression. This seems like a pit at the base of the mountain, but it's actually a spot just below the crest. You can't see the top yet—you think you're nowhere—but you're almost home.[4]

David was well acquainted with sorrow, before and after being made king of Israel. His words in Psalm 23:4 ring familiar to every believer: "Yea, though I walk through the valley of the shadow of death, I will fear no evil: for thou art with me" (KJV). But have we ever stopped to ponder what he really meant? Most of us aren't in danger of losing our lives, as David was, but spiritual burnout can feel like death—at least spiritual death. David's proclamation that God was with him *even in the wilderness* gave him the strength to walk through that dark valley, which seemed to press in from all sides.

This may sound like "bootstrap" therapy—pulling yourself together by your own strength—but it's not. The spiritually burned out person lacks the energy for that. More than anything else, the wilderness phase of our spiritual journey is known for the debilitating sense of inertia it wreaks on weary travelers. What David is doing here is the same thing another, unnamed psalmist did in Psalm 116: "The cords of death entangled me, the anguish of the grave came upon me; I was overcome by trouble and sorrow. Then I called on the name of the LORD: 'O LORD, save me!'" (vv. 3–4 NIV).

These are the words of a desperate man. Beaten down by circumstances, sometimes even by God himself (or so we think), we come to a point in our spiritual journey where all we can do is cry out pathetically, "God, help me!" It's like the white flag of surrender before we succumb to death altogether. Ironically, it's the very point of self-surrender God has been waiting for, the sigh of relinquishment that marks our true readiness to receive his life in us—the Spirit of the living God resonating in our now-emptied wineskins. Remember the lyrics to that old Carly Simon song? *There's more room in a broken heart.* God specializes in filling empty places with his life-giving Spirit.

A few verses later, the psalmist's words have a completely different tone. A transformation has taken place: "Be at rest once more, O my soul, for the LORD has been good to you. For you, O LORD, have delivered my soul from death, my eyes from tears, my feet from stumbling, that I may walk before the LORD in the land of the living" (vv. 7–9 NIV). Reading through the psalm, we may be tempted to think this was a quick change of heart, a revelatory breakthrough of spiritual insight, but in all likelihood the psalmist waded through the wilderness the same way we all do: one dragging step at a time. Only when he reached the other side could he pen the uplifting words we read today.

We have no guarantee that the wilderness phase of our spiritual journey will be swift. It may last only a few months; it may stretch out for years. Only God knows the perfect length of time it takes to get us through to the other side. Believers who find themselves at this most wretched of spiritual way stations can take comfort in the words of Asaph: "But He made His own people go forth like sheep, and guided them in the wilderness like a flock; and he led them on safely, so that they did not fear . . . and He brought them to His holy border" (Ps. 78:52–54a).

Though God may seem silent and far away right now, he is guiding us even in the wilderness. One day we will arrive at those "holy borders" we can only barely glimpse in the distance. Today, Marcia hardly resembles the woman she used to be. It's easy to see that God has wrought a beautiful work of grace in her heart. At the urging of friends, she wrote down her spiritual memoir,[5] had it published, and found healing in telling the tale—as did the protagonists of our next two stories, which center on the sticky problem of spiritual abuse, especially by pastors.

7

The Problem
of Spiritual Abuse

One of the saddest truths about the institutional church, throughout its seventeen-hundred-year history, is the repeated incidence of spiritual abuse by those in leadership. Although the topic of abusive pastors is troubling, this book wouldn't be complete without stories of how some pastors have wounded their flock emotionally, spiritually, and sometimes even physically. It seems baffling that those called to lead God's flock might cause that flock to scatter, to walk away from church—even turn their back on God in some instances. Yet it happens again and again. Jesus stated plainly that his followers were not to lord it over others, like the Roman dictators of the time in which he lived. Rather, he said those who lead must be servants first. Any pastor will acknowledge awareness of this spiritual mandate, and most get it right. The problem centers on a very damaging minority that, I suspect, err because of two things: the fact that they are fallible humans who still war against the flesh (see Rom. 7:21–25) and the history-proven dictum that absolute power corrupts absolutely.

That last item ought to provide insight into why the current CEO model of church government doesn't work. It wasn't supposed to work. Jesus never intended it to happen at all. The body of Christ has embraced a hierarchical system that, in some organizations, spawned during the Middle Ages, resembles royalty, and in others, created in the last century, mirrors corporations. Where along the way did we forget that "pastor" is just one of five ministerial giftings endowed by the Holy Spirit, and that the priesthood of all believers is the design Jesus mandated—in itself a guarantee against predatory leadership?

In *Toxic Faith,* Stephen Arterburn and Jack Felton describe the underbelly of a dictatorial pastor: "Underneath the raging ego of the persecuting leader is a suffering person who fears being unimportant. The position of leadership may have been the first and only time the minister has had any authority. He or she uses the authority to prop up negative feelings of inadequacy. Anyone wanting to advance in the organization must never challenge the authority of the toxic faith leader. Additionally, complete support for the leader and the leader's style of management must also be given without criticism. Any negative comment or action is perceived as a threat that the authoritarian leader cannot handle. The threat is eliminated so the ministry can survive and the mission can be accomplished."[1]

As Arterburn and Felton note, authoritarian leaders come to power because a "driven personality accompanies tremendous talent and charisma." The leader uses persuasive, even manipulative, measures to gain followers' loyalty. "Seeing the dynamic presentation of beliefs and behaviors that are part of the leader's faith, rather than part of true faith in God, the followers willingly accept the teachings, doctrines, and dogma with unquestioning loyalty and allegiance to the leader. The more they accept the teachings of the toxic leader, the more the leader feels the people's dependency, and so the more license the leader takes in controlling the thoughts and beliefs of the followers. As long as people are willing to follow, that leader will feel supposed support from God for ministry and manipulation. The leader is completely unaware that the entire exercise is being conducted to build ego rather than to serve God."[2]

Authority Gone Wrong

Joan, whom we met in chapter 2, says her experience with a corrupt "man of God" as a new believer tainted her view of authority figures in the church. But she weathered the incident and thought that one bad apple shouldn't spoil the whole bushel. What she didn't expect was to encounter controlling or otherwise corrupt leaders two more times in her faith journey. The latter incident—the one that marked her departure from the IC—started out as the best church experience she had ever known.

"When I met a guy who was attending this church, he begged me to try it out one Sunday," Joan recalls. As a member of a church where she struggled to fit in, she welcomed the chance to visit the church her new boyfriend attended.

It was love at first sight, not with the guy (they eventually parted) but with the church. "The church was still kind of small, about a hundred people, but that's what I loved about it. I had attended two megachurches where I felt lost in the crowd. Here, everyone was so friendly, and I immediately felt part of a family."

Joan and her boyfriend went to midweek Bible studies together, served on the worship team, hosted singles gatherings, and even did street evangelism together.

"This is it, I thought. This is what church is supposed to be like," Joan says. The pastor, a warm and caring man, exuded grace and enthusiasm. His evangelistic zeal inspired the people to bring friends and relatives to church services. He taught a "discipleship team" how to share their faith by door-to-door evangelism. Once, when Joan had a private problem, she and her boyfriend sought the pastor's counsel, and he dispensed godly advice in a compassionate manner. Joan grew in her faith and felt sure she had finally found her church home.

A year later, something happened that she now recognizes as the first red flag of warning. A veteran of church fallout, she filed the incident away and decided to give the pastor the benefit of her doubt.

"He had started a new Sunday school class and asked each of us present to sign a statement in our workbooks saying we would faithfully attend every class for that year," she says. "Then we were told to hand our workbooks to our neighbor so they could 'witness' it for us." Such a strict measure seemed unnecessary—and uncalled for—but she went along with it. After all, no one was really expected to object, nor were they asked to think about the matter before "witnessing their signature."

Two weeks later, Joan missed the Sunday school class due to a new medication that caused excessive grogginess; she overslept that morning. "When I walked into church the following week, the pastor smiled and seemed his usual self, but once he started preaching, he hammered on about integrity—about people who say they'll do something and even sign their name to that effect, and then fall through on their promise. I knew instantly he was talking about me. I couldn't believe it."

Other Sundays, his zeal morphed into anger at individuals, and Joan cringed as she recognized the details of a newlywed couple's blended family life in one of the pastor's pulpit stories. One by one the pastor strong-armed his staff and eventually ran off his worship leader, youth leader, men's discipleship leader, and about half the congregation. An older man in the church talked to the pastor privately, encouraging him not to be so authoritarian, but the pastor rebuffed him.

"It got so bad, we were told that for spiritual growth we needed to have a quiet time every day, evangelize every week door to door, have a discipleship leader, attend X number of groups . . . it was exhausting," Joan says. "Several of us met together to discuss what was happening in the church. Every time someone tried to leave, a spiritual SWAT team from the church would go to their house and talk to them, presumably to keep them from leaving. Sometimes they were successful."

Those who left were branded as "out of God's will" or "in rebellion" against spiritual authority. It sounded convincing—especially to the baby Christians in the group. But Joan and several of the other believers recognized spiritual abuse.

"The last Sunday I attended, I was singing with the worship team from the stage, and all of a sudden I thought, 'I can't stay here anymore. This church has become a dangerous place to be spiritually, and it's time to get out.' I wrote a letter to the pastor that next week and told him not to send anyone to my house—I was not backing down on my belief that spiritual abuse was rampant in the church."

Joan did leave and lived in fear for several weeks that the "SWAT team" would pound on her door, demanding to know why she left and using pressure tactics to urge her to return to the fold. But time went by, and she gradually realized she had escaped what turned out to be a near-cultlike congregation. Trying to be a good Christian, she visited church after church but always shrank away from something the pastor said or did from the pulpit platform. After six months, Joan realized she'd become nearly numb from the spiritual disillusionment incurred by her old church. A form of post-traumatic stress syndrome gripped her as she struggled to find a place where she fit in—and where the air of grace flowed freely. Jaded on institutional churches, she finally found fellowship in a

Saturday night gathering of four or five believers who meet to study the Bible, pray, sing, and "just hang out" together over coffee and hors d'oeuvres. "This is church for me now, and I'm thrilled that God finally answered my prayer for a place where I fit."

In spite of the spiritual abuse she's experienced in her life, she says God has wrought an amazing work of grace in her heart. "It's as if the worse people get, the brighter Jesus shines. At some point in the past few years, after I exited that controlling church, I had a real grace awakening. God is more real to me now than he ever was before. The funny thing is, now that the pressure's off to evangelize, I see my light shining brighter than ever before. People are drawn to genuine faith in action—it beams a light into the darkness. I've actually had people approach me and say they can tell by my smile that I've found true contentment. What is my secret, they ask. And then I tell them. Grace really is amazing."

Boundary Breakers

The remarkable thing is that so many believers burned by pastors are still in love with Jesus. Or perhaps it's more correct to say that *because* of their spiritual anguish, they eventually fall into the arms of the living Savior—the same One who told the woman caught in adultery, "Neither do I condemn you; go and sin no more." Some, like Vicki, are living testimonies of grace in the wake of spiritual abuse by a pastor. Raised in a strict denomination, she has a vague recollection of her childhood salvation experience.

"I went to denominational camps every year, read my Bible, had a daily quiet time, went to church, sang in choirs, attended a Christian college—I did all the right things," Vicki says. But still a sense of spiritual vagueness hung over her. At college she met the man she eventually married. Considered a mature Christian, she volunteered as a counselor for a gospel crusade that came to town. "Here I was counseling people on how to become a Christian, but I was just kind of numb," she says. Marriage turned out to be a nightmare, pockmarked with incidents of physical and emotional abuse. She dropped out of church completely for a few years then rejoined the denominational flock at a local church. Throughout her marital ordeal, the words in the Psalms buoyed her foundering spirits. God was reaching out to her, she knows now, but she didn't really take the words to heart.

Despairing over her marriage, Vicki went to her pastor for help. He was young and handsome—and married. During the counseling session he leaned forward across his desk and looked into her eyes. "I'll be for you whatever you need," he said. They struck Vicki as strange words, but she took comfort from them. At least *somebody* seemed to care. The pastor arranged for her to meet him at a restaurant the following day. Over coffee he repeated the words he'd said before, she recalls.

The following week she went to the church for another counseling session. "The pastor came and sat next to me on the sofa, then reached over and put his hand on my knee. I got chills," Vicki says. "He was trying to seduce me. I was married to an abusive husband, and here was an attractive man paying attention to me. It drew me. Within a few days he invited me over to his house on some pretense. His wife was going to be gone for several hours, he said. I must have had some idea of what could happen, but, unbelievably, I went. Twenty minutes later I realized the horror of what was about to happen, and I fled. To this day I thank God for sparing me."

Frightened and confused, Vicki was left with a tarnished view of pastors—and men in general. "I didn't trust them," she says. "And to some degree I felt guilty for letting myself get in that position. Later I found out he had seduced other women in the church. This was the same guy who had counseled me for marital problems and preached about our actions having consequences. I eventually reported him to his denomination, but I don't know what came of it."

Divorced sometime later and living in another city, Vicki still harbored a deep resentment toward the pastor. But, wanting to be a faithful Christian, she became involved in the activities of a large local church, which brought her in contact with several spiritual leaders in diverse roles. Over the years, however, the attitude of those leaders marred her view of Christians and gave her an up-close look at hypocrisy. "They thought they were next to God," she says. "I saw deceitful things going on too. That bothered me. The arrogant attitudes of those leaders started to leave a bad taste in my mouth."

Tired of the big-church programs at her current congregation, Vicki tried a couple of other churches, and "it all just started dying inside me," she says. "I didn't feel like I fit. The whole organized performance, the feeling like you had to do something to measure up to God. I was still begging him to forgive me for everything I'd ever done, and I felt I could never be the person he wanted me to be. I didn't feel worthy of God's love, and I really wasn't comfortable at churches either. I didn't want to go to church anymore."

One afternoon, while at the grocery store, Vicki ran into a young woman she had met at a church function. The woman told her she had bailed out of "regular" church and was now going to a small house gathering that emphasized grace. Desperate, and also curious, Vicki showed up at the next meeting.

"The teaching that night, from a guest speaker, was the most refreshing I'd ever heard," she says. "It was a message of grace. He encouraged us to be with people of similar faith—those who would cheer us on in our walk, not just give us a list of rules to follow. I don't think it's so much that I learned to forgive myself; rather I came to an awareness that God really and truly has forgiven me. By getting that message of grace I was finally able to forgive the abusive pastor and show others the mercy God has shown me."

Vicki says that now she knows why God led her to that small gathering of believers and why the message of grace is so vital to her. "Having grown up in a legalistic environment, this message was so different from anything I'd ever heard. Even though it's the same basic truth of Scripture—that Jesus died for my sins—it's presented in such a refreshing new way. The grace awakening for me was a gradual awareness. Little by little you become more aware of God's love and forgiveness. For the first time in your life, it becomes real to you."

As the saying goes, however, one man's dream is another man's nightmare. In the next chapter we'll discover that the unmerited favor of God can be construed as "greasy grace" to those who perceive spiritual reality through old covenant lenses. The alternative, of course—seeing grace as the "too good to be true" reality that it is—offers the key to the place of rest we all long for.

8

Totally Amazing Grace

Living in Florida, I've witnessed firsthand how powerful brush fires are and how quickly they spread. Driving back from a vacation once, I saw flames in the median of Interstate 95—most likely the result of one spark carried on the wind across the asphalt from the other side of the highway, where a brush fire burned out of control.

Brush fires often start innocuously enough: a stray cigarette coal, spontaneous combustion from the scorching Florida sunlight, or even a bolt of lightning that sets the dry, thirsty undergrowth on fire. And once they start, they're hard to put out.

Wayne, whose story opened this book, likens the good news of the gospel of grace to a spark carried on the wind. He envisions the effect word-of-mouth experiences can have on jaded believers—their spirits barely smoldering—across North America. It all starts with one tiny spark, he says. God fans the spark into flame. That spark jumps across to another believer, ignites his or her spirit [life], then carries "on the wind" to others, changing lives in its wake.

This is not a new gospel (as Paul would say, "God forbid!") but rather a new understanding of what Jesus proclaimed and the apostles set down in the letters that became Scripture.

"Every day I was confessing sins and trying to get right with God," says Wayne. "It got to a point where I said, 'I can't take this anymore.' I was so miserable I was ready to shoot myself or jump off a cliff. All my Christian friends said, 'Hang in there. Grit your teeth! Look at me, I'm happy!' but they looked like they had been baptized in bad vinegar."

Realizing how ineffective the "bootstrap faith" was, Wayne wanted nothing more to do with Christianity, even though he still considered himself a believer. But God was not through with his church-weary prodigal. He showed up in a dramatic way and set Wayne's spirit ablaze through a revelation of grace.

A week after Wayne's disturbing dream about the castle (see chapter 2), he met through a mutual friend a thirty-five-year-old lawyer who had just moved to Orlando from Louisiana. On weekends, groups of singles met to play volleyball and hang out to talk about God and whatever else the conversation rolled into. One night, the attorney, James, showed up at the meeting.

As Wayne recalls, "A bunch of people were discussing how radical it would be for Christians to live together in a first-century-type commune. I remember James sat quietly over in the corner the whole time, just listening. The group talked on and on. Finally somebody said, 'Hey, James, what do you think about all this?' He said, 'If you can have a commune, that's great, but without love you're going to kill each other. Without grace you're going to wind up hurting each other badly.' And then he started to talk about the grace of God—not the doctrine of grace but the spiritual revelation of the finished work of Christ. He talked for about forty-five minutes, and everybody's mouth just sort of dropped open. It was silent in that room."

Wayne knew he had to meet James one-on-one. After the meeting he pulled him aside and told him how miserable he'd been—and how close he'd come to ending it all because of churchianity. James, Wayne, and another man started meeting for breakfast once a week, talking about the grace of God and reading the Scriptures in light of an understanding of grace.

"We'd sit over coffee and talk and talk," Wayne says. "For me, it was almost like being born again all over again. The burden of trying to perform for God was off of me. The understanding kept growing within me. It probably took a few months to get the revelation that my sins weren't held against me, and I felt laughter and joy again. I had years of bad teaching and wrong thinking to undo. I'd sit down with James and Ryan and ask, 'What about this verse? What about that verse?' and we'd hash them out together. For so long the church has taken key verses out of context to make them fit into man's way of thinking. It took about two years of asking and searching before I felt cleansed of the old thinking."

An Organic Work

As he shared with others the reason for his reignited faith, Wayne saw God do an organic work, as he calls it. "The Holy Spirit had planted the seed in these people, and they were blooming. But when true grace is preached, there's going to be controversy. You don't need to raise money to preach the gospel, because the true gospel preached will bring controversy, and the people will come."

Wayne has been labeled a purveyor of easy-believism, greasy grace. But he just waves his hand at the accusations. Like the blind man Jesus healed, he knows he's been set free, he says. Nothing can take that away from him. "What the Ten Commandments could not do, grace comes in and does it all," he says today. "Mercy triumphs over judgment.

Judgment is no longer the issue. In Christianity we have a revelation that the Messiah came and fulfilled the law. What does it mean to fulfill? It means to complete, to finish."

Jesus captured this thought beautifully in John 17:4, where he said, "[Father], I have brought you glory on earth by completing the work you gave me to do" (NIV). What was that work? To take all the law and the prophets and fulfill, in the body of his flesh, the requirement of sin by becoming the final sacrifice, which was pleasing to God.

"It's not a halfway done job. It's complete," Wayne says. "So what's the good news? That I am no longer under the obligation to fulfill the law in my flesh, because he did it. He said in his Word that he's no longer counting my sins against me, because of Jesus. My past, present, and future sins were taken away—not just covered, as they were in the Old Testament—but taken away. John the Baptist didn't say, 'Behold the Lamb of God who covers the sins of the world.' He said, 'Behold the Lamb of God who TAKES AWAY the sins of the world. To proclaim that a man was going to take away our sin was unheard of, even blasphemous. It's why the Pharisees wanted to kill Jesus."

A curious thought: If this is all true, why then do present-day Protestant believers buy into a doctrine that says they must constantly get "right" with God? We can't possibly be more right than we are now, in Christ Jesus. The believers in the churches of Galatia struggled with this very same thing, and the apostle Paul opens the third chapter of his letter to them boldly: "You foolish Galatians! Who has bewitched you? . . . After beginning with the Spirit, are you now trying to attain your goal by human effort?" (Gal. 3:1, 3 NIV).

Wayne points to a handful of authors who are coming out with the same message of God's overwhelming grace. "It's no longer just a doctrine that the church holds, it's now something that is changing people's lives. When people are burnt out, they don't want to hear another doctrine. They say, 'Tell me what it means.' We become ministers of blessing to people."

Riding the Underground Wave

Wayne says he sees the future of the church riding the underground wave that's already surging, back to the house churches and "the steps of the synagogue." Instead of churches buying up new property and constructing buildings, he envisions them going back to the simplistic ways of the first gatherings of believers.

"People are tired of more buildings, more money, more tithing," he says. "Even as we speak there's an underground movement, and it's radical because it's of Christ. For me personally, the end of religion has come. The institutional church, for me, has crumbled. Never again will I attend just to attend. Sunday morning is not sacred to me. Every day that I breathe I am in Christ. I don't have to wait till Sunday to experience the love of God. I can experience it right here at this table in the bookstore café."

For Wayne it all boils down to one word: belief. "It's God's love that compels man to come to repentance, not a building or a list of rules. Think about it: You never hear the apostles say 'Commit!' You never hear them say 'Surrender!' I looked for it; it's not in there. You only ask a hostage to surrender. God does not call us to commit, he calls us to believe in something."

That something is alive and well on planet earth—even in our troubled Western culture—while the shape of how we live out our calling as the body of Christ is undergoing a quiet revolution.

9

On the Steps
of the Synagogue—
or at the Beach

The first hint of fall rustled in the tree leaves as John lifted his coffee mug and gestured toward the natural backdrop of the outdoor café. Behind our table, a small lake sparkled in the early Sunday morning sunshine, and occasional bike riders whizzed past on the athletic trail that circles the lake before heading deep into the meadows and woods beyond. Yes, it was Sunday morning, but neither of us was in church. Instead, we excitedly discussed the unlimited possibilities that thinking out of the "church box" presents. John reminded me of a Scripture verse that God kept dropping into his mind, and we alternately talked about the groundswell of change stirring the religious landscape—Christians who are finding, much to their delight, that the institutional church is not the only way to go about practicing their faith.

When passionate believers weary of churchianity talk about the alternate forms church can take, the canvas is painted with a broad brush. Jesus imposed few rules about how his church should look. And those few rules have more to do with our conduct toward one another than with organizational structure. The church was intended to be an organic, missional community—a radical group of people living on the edge, in the culture but not tainted with the same hue.

"Emerging church," "next-wave church," "ancient-future faith," "postmodern belief," and a slew of other epithets have surfaced as the new buzzwords of this tidal wave of change. But they all boil down to the same thing: with God, the sky is the limit; so too, perhaps, ought our thinking be toward what his body on earth looks like.

Anytime you venture into unfamiliar territory—especially within the church, it seems—the gatekeepers of status quo are ready to pounce and draw the borders in tight around you. But if the church must be in a state of continual reformation, as most Christian thinkers would assert, then we should perpetuate the ongoing conversation of how to make the church relevant as the culture around us changes.

What that means in reality is that some of the options for "church" may seem strange, even controversial, at first glance. In talking with believers hungry for change, I noticed several shocking options emerge. Here are a few, in their own words:

- "It's not a bad thing to take a break from Sunday morning meetings. It's important that people feel wide-open spaces, room for their faith to breathe. And there's no deadline for going back to anything (i.e., the organized church)."
- "Realize that not everything about the institutional church is wrong, but appreciate that everything is back on the table for discussion."

- "Organized religion is putting these definitions on what church is, but the Bible never said, 'You have to go somewhere every Sunday.' Instead, church was meant to be a fluid, interactive, ongoing lifestyle."
- "Find a spiritually mature person (of the same sex) and let them pastor you. The corporate and men's group subcultures already model this mentoring paradigm. Why can't the body of Christ? (Jesus did!)"
- "Jaded believers have been boxed in, and they're searching for the freedom God intended all along. The institution has squelched a lot of great things God has built into his people."
- "It's okay to ask risky questions; it's okay to disagree with a pastor sometimes. We have to give people the ability to think, 'Maybe what I think is right for a change, and the pastor is wrong.'"
- "The institution makes people afraid of possibly stepping into heresy, without 'the covering of a church or pastor,' but being in the institutional church can actually make you more susceptible to heresy because you're taking what other people—or one man/woman—says is the truth, hook, line, and sinker."
- "Parents, instead of abdicating the spiritual teaching of their children to Sunday school, may find themselves stepping up to the plate."
- "Being the church in the culture can mean just about anything—a group of friends gathering over coffee at a bistro; two or three believers playing guitar on the beach and starting conversations about God with curious onlookers; people gathered around a common interest, such as a book discussion group, who find the conversation turning to the spiritual; a camping trip or other outdoor activity with fellow believers (and one or two seekers) that turns into a spiritual retreat in the sanctuary of nature; academic settings, such as seminar

classes, classroom Bible/theology studies, and peer-related discussion groups; Internet discussion groups and chat rooms, where the anonymity of the computer allows people to let down their guard and be real for a while."

One woman said, "What's neat about the online community is that people cherish each other more because of the anonymity—they know their paths might never cross in real life. There are no physical impressions to hinder your friendships and associations. This type of spiritual community is great because you can be so open and honest, and as long as you have someone present who brings it around to a positive note—a 'what are we going to do now?'—it works."

As with any paradigm shift, getting the leaders to back the vision is critical. What often starts as a casual conversation person-to-person gains real momentum for the trajectory once movers and shakers climb aboard. Yet, by its very nature, the new "un-church" movement cringes at the thought of organizing and manipulating others—that's what we're running away from in the institutional church. How much more powerful a belief is when it is birthed by the Holy Spirit and planted in the hearts of leaders and followers alike.

Spencer Burke, a former professional minister and founder of TheOoze.com website, writes about how this transformation took place in his own life:

> For years I've tried to put my finger on it—the reasons why I left the professional pastorate. And you know, more than anything, I think it's this: I left my first love.
>
> The reality is that much of what we call ministry today is really administration. It's about adding things—programs and strategies and rules. In my 22 years as a pastor, I often administered more than I ministered, if that makes sense. I've come to see that I was an add-minister more than a minister. . . .

Nevertheless, it seems I'm a pastor again. My friend Matt and his wife, Krista, are pastors as well. And so is my wife and my five-year-old son, Alden. Yup, we're all pastors at Church.

No, really. That's what it's called: Church. Not First Presbyterian. Not Solomon's Porch or Scum of the Earth or some other cool postmodern name. It's just called Church—and it meets, well, whenever and wherever we decide to meet. Last week it was the park; next week, it might be the beach. . . .

We're breaking pretty much every conventional church-planting rule I know. Why? Because we want to be ministers of the gospel, not 'add-ministers.' We want to be of service, not just a service. . . . But I'd be lying if I said it was easy to let go of the program: it's not. . . .

I've worried about my children. What will happen to them without the safety of an administered Sunday school program. And yet, time and again, they're wowing me with their grasp of the gospel and their ability to understand the heart and soul of Jesus. Will they miss flannelgraphs? Maybe. Only time will tell. I guess.[1]

Burke wraps up his article with this telling statement: "You know, I'm not sure where this is leading. All I know is that my story has taken a new turn. I've joined the 90 percent of the church around the world that doesn't have a paid pastor or a building, but instead, meets in homes, under trees and yes, on California's beaches."[2]

If the emerging church does move out of the sanctuary and back into homes—or on beaches—it will undoubtedly meet with opposition from the organized religious community. Yet as God does an organic work of the Spirit in the hearts of his people, the groundswell can't help but rise until, like a tidal wave, it surges beyond all containment. When that happens, Christianity returns to its original state: a radical way of life that is attractive, compelling, and repelling all at the same time. We were created to be an army of revolutionaries, so why do we more often resemble spectators, watching while a pastor—or a worship team—"does" church for us? Who among us doesn't long for a return to the purity and simplicity of the gospel, as lived out by people possessed of a holy passion! As someone once said, true believers aren't people who have a mission; rather, a mission has them.

Intentional Community

No matter what denomination they hail from or where they fall on the emerging church spectrum, jaded believers all long for the same thing: authentic community. It's the true heart and soul of the church, and without it church is reduced to the dreariest of obligations.

A quiet survey of the emerging church movement reveals that community is increasingly found in creative, hybrid-church settings such as one that has sprung up in downtown Asheville, North Carolina. In this city known as a haven for artists, it's not surprising that a gathering called Soteria (Greek for "salvation") has sprung up in a cavernous nightclub—and attracts believers of every stripe and color.

"What we want to do is have an open forum—a free-form type of worship," says Ernest Hays, who formed Soteria along with his wife, Melody. "It involves celebrating music, dance, theater, visual arts—all the expressionary arts. We want to expose people to things and offer a freedom they'd never get in a regular church." As the *Mountain Xpress* lifestyle news-magazine renders it, "The couple invites folks to just show up at Soteria on weekday evenings and share their talents—a sort of open mic for the Lord. If nobody feels like getting artsy, the Hayses provide coffee and snacks, and people can just hang out and talk."[3]

A writer for a Cincinnati lifestyle weekly describes how one group of believers lives out the call to radical relationship with one another and the community around them.[4] Though these self-proclaimed "Christian anarchists" may teeter left of center for most mainstream believers, their story could be lifted from the pages of the Acts of the Apostles.

The Mustard Seed House Intentional Community, at the time of the article, housed two families who were part of a group of house churches in the area. But the "intentional" community came about by accident. In 1998 Vineyard Central, a church that met at a community center, was given forty-eight hours' notice to vacate when the city condemned the building.

"We panicked and we split into five regional groups and started meeting at people's homes," said Jeremy Drake, one of the Mustard Seed residents. "The pastor would travel around and make sure everybody was on the same page."[5]

When the congregation eventually purchased an abandoned Catholic church, they used the building not for a traditional Sunday morning service but for a Saturday All-Group service for members of the five home groups. Meanwhile, the rectory housed pastors' families while the convent opened its doors to members of Vineyard Central.

"Through all of that we were living on-site and looked around and saw a bunch of people who were either really poor or getting by pretty well, and we decided we should pool our money, just take care of each other," Drake said.

One year later that vision became a reality when the group formed Community House under the same nonprofit status as a monastic society. That building quickly filled to capacity, and so a second facility—the Mustard Seed house—was purchased.

As the article states:

On Sunday mornings the housemates pile into a car and head off to worship, but not at a church. They are part of a growing House Church movement, in which groups of three or more meet in homes to worship without the trappings of an organized service.

House churches have been popping up across the United States as Christians look for a hands-on alternative to organized religion. The house church movement strives to de-program the church and strip it back down to its base elements.

"The American church, because of its market-driven concepts and its corporate mentality, has basically been co-opted by corporate America," Bell says. . . . "We've really lost our first task, which is to make disciples and the only way you can do that is through intimate relations with one another and sharing your life through some sort of faith community. . . . It's just about support. Relationships. It's not really about organizations."[6]

For many jaded believers, it is that very "corporateness" of the institutional church that has soured them on Sunday mornings. How did we get so far from the original blueprint, they collectively wonder, even if they've never experienced anything like the early church.

A September 2003 story by *Forbes* magazine reports that megachurches in North America have indeed become mega-businesses, with pastors filling the powerful role of chief executive officers who "use business tactics to grow their congregations."

Referring to one megachurch, Lakewood Church in Houston, the article asserts: "As for the services themselves, Lakewood makes sure to put on a grand show. It has a 12-piece stage band, a lighting designer to set the mood and three large projection screens. The technology will be even more spectacular when it moves into its new home in the former Houston Rockets' stadium."

Forbes summarizes: "No doubt, churches have learned some valuable lessons from corporations. Now maybe they can teach businesses a thing or two." And certainly if you queried members of these rapidly growing megachurches—along with their vibrant small and midsize sister churches—you'd find believers who wouldn't dream of doing church any other way.

Their faith has deepened by being part of these congregations. They've encountered Christ through relationships with other believers and found community through participation in ministries or small groups.

We are left with the question: If the corporate/organizational church structure works so well for some believers, why does it leave others cold? What is the trigger that marks their departure from the institutional ranks? Is it a picky, disgruntled nature? A rebel-yell attitude? A reluctance to be categorized? Or is something deeper and more heartfelt at work in their spirits?

Sour apples will emerge in every bushel (and if we're honest, most of us have been one at some time or another), so it seems unfair to dismiss an entire movement—that of the emerging church—by labeling its respective members rebels. Again, we must look long and hard at the fruit of this spiritual groundswell, checking it for the telltale signs of Christlikeness.

The apostle Paul wrote to the young church at Ephesus, and to us as fellow believers:

> I urge you to live a life worthy of the calling you have received. Be completely humble and gentle; be patient, bearing with one another in love. Make every effort to keep the unity of the Spirit through the bond of peace. . . . To each one of us grace has been given as Christ apportioned it. . . . It was he who gave some to be apostles, some to be prophets, some to be evangelists, and some to be pastors and teachers, to prepare God's people for works of service, so that the body of Christ may built up until we all reach unity in the faith and in the knowledge of the Son of God and become mature, attaining to the whole measure of the fullness of Christ.
>
> Ephesians 4:1–3, 7, 11–13 NIV

Like church reformers before us, we must stick to the truth of Scripture and let it be our guide—even when it overturns centuries or mere decades of religious tradition. Belief, and the quiet revelation of truth the Holy Spirit brings to individual Christians, is indeed the hallmark of the Christian faith. Things started out so simply and purely for the early church, but—seen from the vantage point of history—it didn't take long for the train to veer off the track. One man, convinced of the truth in the privacy of his monastic cell, would steer it back on course.

10

LUTHER'S LEGACY

Thunderstorms brewing in the skies of a summer day have always intrigued me. I remember my introduction as a child to that eerie calm before the storm when the air is at once still and yet humming with expectancy. You and all of nature seem to know: Something big is about to happen. Even the cicadas have gone silent. Somewhere between stillness and fury, the humid summer air begins to stir, blowing suddenly cooler.

One such summer day I watched my mother's face as she gazed out our kitchen window to the backyard, where freshly washed sheets and towels started to dance on the wind. "Quick, grab the extra laundry basket and come with me!" It was a command, not a request, and the lines of worry creased on her brow made my footsteps a bit faster. As we hurried outside with our plastic baskets, my mother's eyes darted at the trees, which had begun their own peculiar dance.

"When I was little, they used to say you could tell a thunderstorm was coming when the backs of the leaves showed," she said as we hurried toward the line and started snapping still-damp sheets off the wire. The wind was hissing now, scattering bits of debris against my bare legs. A cool wet towel wrapped around my face from the force of the wind, and I shook it away to work faster, glancing at the trees as I did. The leaves showed their backs all right, and the woods that marched up to the boundary of our domestic North Carolina plot twisted with the expectation of the coming storm.

Only a half hour before I had been playing calmly in this same backyard, the air hanging warm and languid as a blanket around me. Now the air had taken on a life of its own, carrying a message of foreboding and excitement at the same time. Minutes later, while watching the storm unleash its power from behind the relative safety of our living room windowpanes, I had my first memorable glimpse of God in action. What else could wreak such havoc and beauty at the same time?

A Troubled Monk

In the early sixteenth century, a similar storm was brewing over the spiritual landscape of Europe, and an obscure German monk who dedicated himself to the study of Scripture pored over a troubling passage from Paul's letter to the Romans. Martin Luther, perhaps history's most famous "jaded believer," was weary from churchianity too, but it was no garden variety dullness that planted a seed of divine discontent inside his spirit. The corrupt Roman Catholic Church of his day required worshippers to pay fees (indulgences) for their sins to be forgiven. Luther, alternately labeled a hero and a heretic, became the unwitting catalyst of the church's most significant shakeup since the Day of Pentecost. And though he was a controversial figure endowed with his fair share of flaws, he is nonetheless credited with turning history on its ear.

As one historical website puts it, "Luther . . . often called himself a simple monk or a simple Christian. He marveled that a straightforward stand of conscience had turned him into one of the most-talked-about people of his time. Yet that simple Christian and that simple stand of conscience started an ecclesiastical shock wave that changed the course of Western history."[1]

Oddly, it was a thunderstorm that triggered Luther's initial search for godliness as a young man. On the road home from visiting his parents, Luther was flung to the ground as a lightning bolt struck the earth nearby. Shaken to the core, he vowed to become a monk if God spared his life. That same month he entered a monastery. Ordained to the priesthood, Luther was charged with the task of journeying to Rome to handle some of his order's political affairs. The Roman pilgrimage proved to be the spark that kindled a growing disillusionment with the church he professed to love.

> When I made my pilgrimage to Rome, I was such a fanatical saint that I dashed through all the churches and crypts, believing all the stinking forgeries of those places. . . . I know priests who said six or seven Masses while I said only one. They took money for them and I didn't. . . . Whoever came to Rome with money received the forgiveness of sins. Like a fool, I carried onions to Rome and brought back garlic. . . . I wouldn't take one thousand florins for not having seen Rome because I wouldn't have been able to believe such things if I had been told by somebody without having seen them for myself.[2]

Troubled by the church's corrupt status, Luther nonetheless made good on his vow and lived the harsh, ascetic life of a monk-priest. "I was a devout monk and wanted to force God to justify me because of my works and the severity of my life," he later wrote. "I was a good monk, and kept the rule of my order so strictly that I may say that if ever a monk got to heaven by his monkery, I would have gotten there as well. . . . I was very pious in the monastery, yet I was sad because I thought God was not gracious to me."[3]

Something was missing, and Luther wrestled with the words of Scripture to find out what it was. Eventually his sadness turned into rage against God: "As if, indeed, it is not enough, that miserable sinners, eternally lost through original sin, are crushed by every kind of calamity by the law of the Decalogue, without having God add pain to pain by the gospel and also the gospel threatening us with his righteousness and wrath!"[4]

A doctor of theology at the University of Wittenberg, Luther began a year-long series of lectures on Paul's epistle to the Romans in May 1515. As he studied, one phrase kept turning in his mind: "In it the righteousness of God is revealed, as it is written, 'He who through faith is righteous shall live.' " Well-versed in St. Augustine's writings about salvific grace, Luther "beat importunately upon Paul at that place, most ardently desiring to know what St. Paul wanted."

His desire was rewarded. Owing his breakthrough insights to a revelatory reading of Scripture, Luther came to the conclusion that guaranteed him a place in history and rocked the religious and social world of his day: The just shall live by faith.

> At last, by the mercy of God, meditating day and night, I gave heed to the context of the words. . . . There I began to understand that the righteousness of God is that by which the righteous lives by a gift of God, namely by faith. And this is the meaning: the righteousness of God is revealed by the gospel, namely, the passive righteousness with which merciful God justifies us by faith, as it is written, "He who through faith is righteous shall live." Here I felt altogether born again and had entered paradise itself through open gates. There a totally other face of the entire Scripture showed itself to me. Thereupon I ran through the Scripture from memory. I also found in other terms an analogy, as, the work of God, that is what God does in us, the power of God, with which he

110

makes us wise, the strength of God, the salvation of God,
the glory of God.

And I extolled my sweetest word with a love as great as
the hatred with which I had before hated the word "righteousness of God." Thus that place in Paul was for me truly
the gate to paradise.[5]

An outspoken critic of the selling of indulgences, Luther
had already earned powerful enemies in the church. Two years
later, on All Hallows' Eve (October 31), he tacked his famous
95 theses to the door of the Wittenberg Castle Church, which
served as a bulletin board for the university. Intending to spur
debate, he initially got very little response, but once word of
his theses got out, the storm gathered strength.

By 1521, after a series of escalating events and charges of
heresy from Rome, Luther was tried in an imperial court
before the emperor. Asked to recant, he stated, "Unless I am
convinced by Scripture and plain reason—I do not accept the
authority of popes and councils, for they have contradicted
each other—my conscience is captive to the Word of God.
I cannot and will not recant anything, for to go against conscience is neither right nor safe. God help me."[6]

Birth of a Revolution

Once set into motion, change swept across the church
landscape of middle Europe. While in hiding for his life at
Wartburg Castle, Luther heard that the town of Wittenberg
itself had changed. By 1522 monks refused to say private
Mass and began leaving the Augustinian congregation until it
was completely disbanded. The minister at the castle church
married. Students destroyed the altar at the Franciscan monastery. Most shocking of all, an evangelical Lord's Supper
was now celebrated with the liturgy in German and the cup
offered to the laity. In a document about the Mass, Luther

111

expressed his wish that the sacred ritual be celebrated solely in the vernacular, accessible to the common people. He called on poets and musicians of his day to develop the appropriate settings for that transition.

Though his bold stand of conviction overturned centuries of bad teaching, Luther knew how costly the truth was. Word reached him that on July 1, 1523, the first Protestant martyrs had been burned in Brussels. The Protestant Reformation was born, and the price was high indeed.

Today we read the account of Luther as any other textbook rendering of history-shaping events. But imagine what it must have been like to live them. Imagine what boldness it took to make a life-or-death stand against the organized clergy, the omnipotent Roman Church of the Middle Ages. We flip through our history books and read that Luther's radical stance carved a schism in the timeline of world events, separating the Middle Ages from the dawning of spiritual, social, and creative light known as the Renaissance.

For a little while, the world had forgotten the treasures of heaven Paul wrote about when he addressed the young church at Ephesus. As the commentary in *The Open Bible* (NKJV) renders it: "Ephesians is addressed to a group of believers who are rich beyond measure in Jesus Christ, yet living as beggars, and only because they are ignorant of their wealth. Since they have yet to accept wealth, they relegate themselves to living as spiritual paupers. Paul begins by describing . . . the contents of the Christian's heavenly 'bank account': adoption, acceptance, redemption, forgiveness, wisdom, inheritance, the seal of the Holy Spirit, life, grace, citizenship—in short, every spiritual blessing. Drawing upon that huge spiritual endowment, the Christian has all the resources needed for living 'to the praise of the glory of His grace.'"

Paul could have been talking about us. Born into such a rich inheritance—the sons and daughters of a King—we settle for a pauper's life spiritually, slogging along and hoping we'll bump into the abundant life someday. Like Luther centuries later, Paul "beat importunately" upon the believers at Ephesus, praying that "the God of our Lord Jesus Christ, the Father of glory, may give to you the spirit of wisdom and revelation in the knowledge of Him, *the eyes of your understanding being enlightened;* that you may know what is the hope of His calling, what are the riches of the glory of His inheritance in the saints, and what is the exceeding greatness of His power toward us who believe" (Eph. 1:17–19a, emphasis mine).

Perhaps the most memorable scene in Disney's animated film *The Lion King* occurs when Simba, a young prince of a lion, is banished from the den by an evil interloper. His father has been killed, and Simba is emotionally and physically lost. On the advice of a mystical baboon, Simba gazes into a pool of clear water and sees a vision of his father, the former king. "Simba," his father's voice intones, "remember who you are!"

"You see," cries the baboon, Rafiki, "he lives in you!"

Do we remember who we are "in Christ"? Have we traded the simplicity of the gospel of grace for a works theology, though we talk about grace freely? Writing to the young churches in central Asia Minor, Paul said, "But now after you have known God, or rather are known by God, how is it that you turn again to the weak and beggarly elements, to which you desire again to be in bondage? . . . Stand fast therefore in the liberty by which Christ has made us free, and do not be entangled again with a yoke of bondage. . . . You ran well. Who hindered you from obeying the truth? This persuasion [being under the law] does not come from Him who calls you" (Gal. 4:9; 5:1, 7–8).

Jesus said if we seek the truth we will find it, and the truth will set us free. Surprisingly, the truth was right under our noses the whole time—read from the Scriptures again and again—but many of us missed it because of our culture's collective attachment to a program-centered belief. The final story in this book describes what happened to one jaded believer after he traded a formulaic approach to Christianity for spiritual realism. Or rather, what happened when he *remembered who he was in Christ.*

11

A Second Reformation?

James, the attorney we first met in chapter 8, couldn't shake the feeling that something was missing. Raised in a liturgical Protestant church, he nonetheless sensed an unidentified longing in his soul that the ritual could not satisfy. As a teenager he'd watch Billy Graham crusades on TV and feel a tug in his spirit. "Sometimes I'd walk outside after watching them and cry under the trees in our backyard," he says. "God was calling me, but I didn't know how to get to him."

One evening he watched a beautiful sunset stretch across the horizon and wished his girlfriend could be there to share it with him. In the stillness, he sensed a voice inside his spirit saying: "I wish you wanted to share that sunset with me."

"That moment turned a switch in me," James recalls. "Up to this point, I had basically used God to get what I wanted. Now he started asking me questions; he started working on the inside of me." The calling grew stronger day by day. "I'd go out dancing in nightclubs and hear the song 'Nights in White Satin' over the sound system. It was like God speaking to me—I love you, oh, how I love you! It got to the point where I knew I had to do something." Billy Graham urged people to profess their faith in Christ publicly, so James called the pastor of another local church (one that gave altar calls) and told him he wanted to walk down the aisle that Sunday morning. Sitting in the back of the church, he clenched his hands to keep them from shaking. "It was a big step, but I was ready for whatever God wanted to do with me," he says. "That day I was truly born of the Spirit. After that, everything began to take off."

A student at Louisiana State University, he joined a non-denominational fellowship that sprang out of a coffeehouse ministry and attracted the college crowd. The pastor, a physician by trade, took no salary from the ministry—modeling for James how a person could be both a professional and a minister of the gospel without being a clergyman. It was a pattern he himself would emulate years later.

From the beginning James loved to teach the Scriptures and tell others about what God was doing in his life. That passion for the Word of God consumed him, even while he studied long hours to become a lawyer. And, like so many other believers, he says, "I had this mixture of law and grace. I didn't yet see the whole picture of what Jesus did on the cross."

Ten years later he reached a burnout point. "After a decade of working hard for God and trying to please God—never resting, never meeting expectations—you just get weary," he says. "You think, Where's life? Does the Christian battery give out after ten years? I didn't want to hear another Christian tape, read the Bible, or even go to church. I dropped out."

Having thrown off the church's shackles, James went out and partied, but a peculiar thing started to happen. Now he looked at the world through different eyes—he saw people in a whole new light. "Before, I looked at nonbelievers through religious eyes. I was always ready with a Scripture, but I didn't really see them as they were. Little by little, a lot of religious baggage started dropping off me. I felt I had left the church, but God never left me." A self-described poor listener, he found himself really listening to people. Instead of offering knee-jerk Christian responses to people's problems and missing what they were really saying, he often admitted he didn't have a clue.

"The presence of God became more real to me as I became more real," he says. "There was a new simplicity and realism about my life. At the same time I felt his love. It's always been his love that drew me. This time I felt God's love drawing me back to himself."

A friend gave James a tape that featured the song "When God Ran." The song describes the only time in Scripture where God the Father is depicted as running—toward the prodigal son, toward us. "Here's the legalistic brother who wouldn't go out to meet the prodigal, but the father is hoisting up his robes and running out to meet his son," he says. "That parable helped me begin to come back to God. In a sense I was never a real prodigal because I didn't reject God; I had just left the fold—the institutional church."

A "New" Thing

Recharged with a spiritual zeal, James spent hours contemplating the Scriptures and felt especially drawn to comparisons between the Old and New Testaments. He sensed God telling him to study what the "mystery of Christ" was. "I went to a Christian bookstore and looked at all the commentaries where Paul talked about the subject, but I felt that God was saying, No, that's not it; no, that's not it. Paul was describing something revolutionary—something that had not even been revealed to the sons of men prior [to Christ]."

To gain insight into the true meaning of the new covenant, James listened to messages being preached from pulpits and heard the Spirit whisper, *Which of these messages could* not *have been preached before Jesus came?* But of the Sunday morning messages he heard, almost everything could have been preached before Christ, under the old covenant.

"I heard them talking about the fear of God, obeying commandments, pleasing God, that God is holy and man is sinful," he says. "Jesus was thrown in every now and then, but it was like a warmed-over Old Testament theology with a bit of New Testament added in—nothing that sounded like a mystery. Nothing new. Yet the Scriptures say that when Jesus came it would be entirely new. 'Behold I do a new thing. Consider not the things of old,' the prophets proclaimed. Ask most believers what the difference is between the Old and New Testaments, and they won't really have a distinction, other than the sacrifice of lambs and goats instead of Jesus. God teaches by contrasts, so if we think Old and New are basically the same, then we're not getting it."

In his Scripture study, James looked anew at the Gospel of John. The "beloved apostle" records Jesus as saying, "He who hears My word and believes in Him who sent Me has everlasting life, and shall not come into judgment, but has [already] passed from death into life" (John 5:24). "I began to see that this is huge—it's a huge contrast from the old covenant," James says. "As believers, we've already passed through judgment. The story of Noah is really a foreshadowing of Christ. Noah was brought through the waters of judgment to a new land, a new beginning. I began to bask in the realization that *judgment is over for the believer.* The unbeliever is still in his sin. The same judgment was accomplished at the cross, but each individual has to receive it. God sacrificed the Lamb, but we have to receive the Lamb. No sin is too bad for anybody to miss heaven. The only sin that will send someone to hell is rejecting Christ. Jesus took all our sin. The real sin is the sin of unbelief."

Once a believer understands the true nature of grace, phrases such as "Christ in us the hope of glory" become a reality, James says. "Basically the mystery is Christ revealed—his death, burial, and resurrection. Through his Son, God was going to judge the whole human race and raise a new creation. The cross would be the end of Adam's race and the beginning of a new [spiritual] race. Everyone who receives the Spirit has a new heart; that was the promise spoken in the prophets—that God would sprinkle us and give us a new heart."

For several years James taught the Bible at a small gathering of believers. Today, he meets with other believers whenever he can, and the conversation always turns to his favorite topic: the mystery of Christ in us.

"If I felt God leading me [to an institutional church], I wouldn't be opposed to it," he says. "God can lead you some places to be a light. But right now so many things are foundationally wrong with the church that I would cause trouble. I'd rather just meet with a group of friends in a home somewhere."

James believes the organized church today espouses some seriously flawed teachings, namely an unhealthy focus on sin. Contrary to much pulpit teaching today, he asserts, the Spirit is not intent on exposing our sins—to us or to others. The sin issue for the entire human race was dealt with almost two thousand years ago. The Spirit's mission from heaven is to reveal Jesus, the righteousness of God given freely to all who believe on him. If that is the Spirit's mission, why would he be interested in bringing up that which is part of the old man that God considers dead? The Spirit has been given to reveal the deep things of God, not the deep things of our flesh. We know that no good thing dwells in our flesh, so we are not to look there for anything that could possibly give us life. As God said in the beginning to Adam, "Who told you that you were naked?" It is not God's way to show us our nakedness in order to transform us. Yes, initially, we must see that we are naked, but once we are clothed with Christ, the Father shows us Christ continually, not our former nakedness.

119

Yet, being human, we still feel the weakness of our humanity. As Paul said, "We have this treasure in earthen vessels." That is part of God's plan also, it seems. Our life as a new creation—a person born of the Spirit—works through a dependence on God, because apart from Christ we can do nothing.

Even when we feel down, we need never lose the awareness of our union with Christ. "It's not about trying to be like the old mystics who went off to find union with God," James asserts. "We already have union with God, with no help from the church. The [organized] church's whole emphasis is to show us our sin, as opposed to reveal Christ to us. We think the way a person is transformed spiritually is by focusing on sin and confessing sin. The dynamic that changes lives and sets us free is all about, as Paul said, setting your mind on things above. The mind set on things above—the spiritual realities, the new things the Spirit reveals to us—is how we walk in the Spirit."

The apostolic way of transformation is beholding Christ—focusing on Jesus, not our sin. As James proclaims to everyone who will listen, "When you see him and who you are in him, you no longer 'see' your flesh. Behind all this is a very personal God who just loves you. You can't experience that true love unless you see what he has wrought. Believers today are being told they're not right with God and all these things that block the light of seeing they are beloved of God. That's why so many people get discouraged and give up. You can't 'see' that reality with the mind-set preached in most churches today. But this is why the gospel is so awesome. It's transforming. It's phenomenal. Once you grasp what Christ did for us, it literally explodes within you. Martin Luther brought a lot back. The whole church was trapped in legalism. He restored a lot of truth to the church, but we need another reformation to bring us all the way back to the simplicity of Christ. It's long overdue."

It seems cruelly simplistic to say "get grace!" to believers so jaded they're paralyzed with spiritual inertia. Yet, in nearly every story contributed to this book, the person's stumblings through the wilderness led to a stripped-down faith bereft of church trappings and the "Christian" masks we so easily don, until they too became rock-bottom believers—dwellers of that strange middle earth between belief and cynicism, a place of knowing the truth of God yet despairing of its personal validity until it hits you broadside with a realism that outstrips every Sunday school lesson you ever learned. Just when these jaded believers thought they could sink no lower, just when God seemed more remote and careless than ever, his love broke through, meeting them in the wilderness and exchanging their spiritual deadness for the abundant life only he can give.

Abundant life doesn't mean a state of perpetual happiness, I've discovered. And surely not every believer takes the same route on their faith-walk. In fact, it's not a journey we could map out even if we chose, as though the task of creating a spiritual itinerary could help us "arrive" when and where we desired. Rather, this lifelong journey—at once wonderful, troubling, and mysterious—is a sojourn God crafts for us, sometimes at odds with our own plans and always at great cost, once our heart cries out to know him more. Amazingly, God starts us down this path even when that heart-cry is so faint we can't hear it ourselves.

Above all else, the abundant life of Jesus Christ is marked by rest—a spiritual rest that seems almost oxymoronic in our frenzied world: Rest in the knowledge that God will shine a lamp showing us the next step to take; rest in the knowledge that his timing is always maddeningly perfect; rest in the knowledge that our frettings and worryings can't make anything right; rest in the knowledge that he is for us when the whole world seems to be against us; rest in the knowledge that we don't have to "be good" to make him love us; rest in the knowledge that nothing we can do will chase his love away; rest in the knowledge that we'll blow it every time we try to take things into our own hands (so why try anyway?—yet we do); and rest in the knowledge that the God of the universe longs to see us face to face in a place that outstrips our wildest imaginings.

No amount of striving can catapult a spiritually weary soul into the place of bright belief, but God can. As we let him water the tiny seeds of faith in our hearts—no matter how trampled down they are—something green and growing begins to take root. That something is a full-bodied knowing with every fiber of our being that the grace of God reached down to save us too.

At the time of the Corinthian epistles, the Judaizers came behind Paul's teaching and tried to hold everyone captive to the Law of Moses, wrecking the gospel. Paul exerted so much energy setting people free from the law because he saw the mystery of grace. No wonder he said in the Book of Galatians that he travailed as of one giving birth (see Gal. 4:19). Once believers are free from the law they can begin to see the reality of Christ. They are free to break out of centuries-old traditions and reclaim a first-century faith. When that happens to you and me—and every other believer who yearns to run behind the Good Shepherd on the high green hills—then it will be said of us, as it was said of the apostles, "Those who have turned the world upside down have come here too" (Acts 17:6).

And who could doubt that our world is ripe for being turned upside down?

Afterword

I began this book by comparing our spiritual journeys to that of a wayfarer striking out on a trail—and giving an account of the trip when they return. Like physical travelers, no two spiritual sojourners will have the exact same story to tell, but they may find many similarities when they compare notes with fellow travelers. Chief among those common points in *Jaded* is a divine discontent, a general weariness with the institutional church, and a yearning for something more than programs. The fact that this refrain keeps cropping up across North America doesn't make it right or wrong; this book is simply a record of what is happening.

My primary concern in writing *Jaded* was that those in church leadership would cry foul (or even "mutiny!") and sense a dagger mind-set imbedded in the text. The first concern may be inevitable; as to the second, nothing could be further from the truth. Along with myself, the people who contributed their stories to this book love the church—meaning the body of Christ—and long to see it restored. What shape or form that restoration ultimately takes remains for Jesus, the Author and Finisher of our faith, to work out.

And, if the record of Scripture is any clue, God is a master at surprise plot twists and creative endings.

Over the next few decades, the church of the twenty-first century may come to resemble its oldest cousin—the early church led by the apostles, meeting in homes and on the "steps of the synagogues"—or it could morph into something we've never quite seen before in history. One thing we know for sure: The church is God's idea, and we're bound to one another in Christ, for better or worse. It was his idea that believers hang out together, open the Scriptures together, break bread together, and even appoint leaders among their ranks. But perhaps the way we go about "organizing" all of the above is what so desperately needs overhauling.

Inherent dangers lurk anytime believers try to live a Lone Ranger existence, apart from other Christ-followers. We need each other. As one concerned pastor urged me during the writing of this book, we must love the church "even in all her whoreness" and leave the results up to God. Scripture promises that the good work Jesus began in us he will bring to completion (see Philippians 1:6). What powerful words! He *will* bring us—a collective, imperfect herd of wandering, blemished sheep—into his Father's sheepfold. We can rest in the knowledge. And whenever someone asks us about our own spiritual journey with the Savior, wanting to know, What was it like? Whom did you meet along the way? Was the terrain difficult? *Was it worth the trip?* we can have the boldness to say: This is one journey you don't want to miss.

Πotes

Chapter 1   Rock-Bottom Believers

1. Philip Yancey, *Soul Survivor: How My Faith Survived the Church* (New York: Doubleday, 2001), 6.

2. Frank Peretti, *The Visitation* (Nashville, Tenn.: Word, 1999), 67, 148.

Chapter 2   Call Me Ishmael

1. Dietrich Bonhoeffer, *The Cost of Discipleship* (New York: Macmillan Publishing, 1963), 99.

2. Amy Mandelker and Elizabeth Powers, eds., *Pilgrim Souls: A Collection of Spiritual Autobiographies* (New York: Simon & Schuster, 1999), 540–41.

Chapter 3   The Church's Back Door

1. George Barna and Mark Hatch, *Boiling Point: Monitoring Cultural Shifts in the 21ˢᵗ Century* (Ventura, Calif.: Regal Books, 2001), 212–13.

2. Ibid.

3. Robert Wuthnow, *Christianity in the 21ˢᵗ Century: Reflections on the Challenges Ahead* (New York: Oxford University Press, 1993), 39.

4. Excerpted from http://www.orthovox.org/orthovox/conxnty.htm

5. Ibid.

6. Barna and Hatch, *Boiling Point,* 239.

7. Brian D. McLaren, *A New Kind of Christian* (San Francisco: Jossey-Bass, 2001), xv.

Chapter 4   What Is This Thing Called Church?

1. In his book *Paul: A Novel* (Zondervan, 2000), Walter Wangerin depicts the apostle Paul as a small man. I've taken the liberty to borrow that physical likeness here.

2. Excerpted from the article "The House Church Movement" by Loren Smith, www.homechurch.org

3. Ibid.

4. Ibid.

5. Tracey Amino, "Help! My House Church Is Worse Than the Institutional Church Ever Was!" www.homechurch-homepage.org.

6. Ibid.

7. Andrew Jones, "My Gripes about the House Church Movement," January 2003, Ncubator Internet Resources.

8. Excerpted from the article "Caution—Steps Toward Denominationalism" by Nate Krupp, www.radchr.net

9. Ibid.

10. Ibid.

Chapter 5   From Religion 101 to Spirituality.com

1. Barna and Hatch, *Boiling Point,* 214.

2. George Barna, *The Second Coming of the Church* (Nashville, Tenn.: Word, 1998), 19.

3. Brenda Brasher, *Give Me That Online Religion* (San Francisco: Jossey-Bass, 2001), 44.

Chapter 6   Working Hard at Being Good

1. Quoted in Smith, "The House Church Movement," www.home church.org.

2. Stephen Arterburn and Jack Felton, *Toxic Faith* (Nashville, Tenn.: Thomas Nelson, 1991).

3. Ibid., 177–78.

4. Thomas Whiteman and Randy Petersen, *Your Marriage and the Internet* (Grand Rapids: Revell, 2002).

5. Marcia Ford, *Memoir of a Misfit* (San Francisco: Jossey-Bass, 2003).

Chapter 7   The Problem of Spiritual Abuse

1. Arterburn and Felton, *Toxic Faith,* 170.
2. Ibid., 170–71.

Chapter 9   On the Steps of the Synagogue—or at the Beach

1. Excerpted from "A Church with No Name" by Spencer Burke, www.theooze.com
2. Ibid.
3. Marsha Barber, "The Spirit of the Streets," *Mountain Xpress,* November 19, 2003.
4. Excerpted from "Get with the De-Program" by Rebecca Lomax, Cincinnati CityBeat, http://www.citybeat.com/2001-10-18/ news .shtml
5. Ibid.
6. Ibid.

Chapter 10   Luther's Legacy

1. Excerpted from www.susanlynnpeterson.com/luther/home
2. Mandelker and Powers, *Pilgrim Souls: A Collection of Spiritual Autobiographies,* 167–68.
3. Ibid., 167.
4. Ibid., 169.
5. Ibid.
6. www.luther.de

A. J. Kiesling is the author of several books, including *Live Like a Jesus Freak* and *Soul Deep: Prayers & Promises for Cultivating Inner Beauty.* She has worked as a writer and editor in the Christian publishing industry since 1985 and is a freelance religion reporter for *Publishers Weekly.* To share your thoughts or comments on *Jaded,* email her at jaded0351@yahoo.com.